MISSION CRITICAL MESSAGES

How to Create a Global Impact

TRACY REPCHUK
with
Deanna Hansen | Marci Baun | Rose Phan | Hugh Campbell | Javier Guerrero | Annette Fazio
Tonya Hoffman | Mari Muscio | Bonnie Bradford | Kim Dandurand | Mary Stevenson

Other Works with Tracy Repchuk

 **Start Right Marketing**

31 Days to Millionaire Marketing Miracles

 **The Poetry of Business**

Quantum Leap Your Life

 **Ultimate Life Lessons**

25 Brilliant Business Mentors

 **Ready, Aim, Inspire**

Empower Business Everywhere

Discover more at
http://TracyRepchuk.com

Mission Critical Messages
How to Create a Global Impact

Tracy Repchuk

Co-authored with

Deanna Hansen • Marci Baun • Rose Phan
Hugh Campbell • Javier Guerrero
Annette Fazio • Tonya Hofmann
Mari Muscio • Bonnie Bradford
Kim Dandurand • Mary Stevenson

QuantumLeapAuthor.com

Published by QuantumLeapAuthor.com
Burbank, California

First published printing, March 2016

Copyright © 2016 by Tracy Repchuk
All Rights Reserved

No part of the book may be used, reproduced, uploaded, or transmitted by any means (including electronic, mechanical, recording, or otherwise) without the prior written permission of the publisher and individual co-authors, with the exception of brief quotations for written reviews or articles. No copying, uploading, or distribution of this book via the Internet is permissible.

The author, writers, and publisher have made every effort to include accurate information and website addresses in this work at the time of publication, and assume no responsibility for changes, omissions, inaccuracies, or errors that occur before or after publication.

ISBN-10: 1523980575
ISBN-13: 978-1523980574

Business & Money - International - Global Marketing
Business & Money - Business Culture - Work Life Balance

Printed in the United States of America

Cover Images:
Copyright: Innersurf International

For more information, or to order bulk copies of this book, please contact QuantumLeapAuthor.com or
Tracy Repchuk at http://TracyRepchuk.com.

Dedication and Acknowledgements

I would like to dedicate this book to those who are doing whatever it takes to get your mission critical message out to the world. It's never easy when you go against what has become 'normal' or an 'accepted' state of society, despite how crazy it will seem to you, because normal never is.

Normal has become drugging children, the elderly, and anyone in between for anything you can think of—mandated vaccinations, GMO based foods, lobotomies to treat the 'insane', but change is a comin'. Organic, natural, spiritual, drug free, restored education, promotion of positive stories, change, people, news, empowering women, causes and others, overcoming disabilities and obstacles, philanthropy, forgiveness, eradication of crime, war, poverty, movements towards peace on earth—and all of it is possible in our lifetime.

In addition, I'd like to thank those who support them—so we can lead, participate, and connect with amazing people, just like you. When we have support from family, friends, associates, mentors, coaches, mastermind groups, and followers, it gives us the luxury of time to do projects like this.

Special acknowledgements to those who have become a special part of my journey, learning, and respect:

Bernie Dohrmann, Ellen DeGeneres, James H. Stern, Laura Herring, Les Brown, Mark Zuckerberg, Meg Whitman, Michelle Patterson, Napoleon Hill, Nick Vujicic, Rudy Ruettiger, Seth Godin, Shawne Duperon, and Steve Jobs.

Enjoy the book and connect with each of us!
Tracy Repchuk, 7 Time #1 International Bestselling Author and Speaker

Contents

Foreword 11

Chapter 1
Identifying Your Mission Critical Messages
by Tracy Repchuk 13

Chapter 2
The Health Crisis of the Youth—And the Solution
by Deanna Hansen 23

Chapter 3
Write Your Story that will Change the World
by Marci Baun 29

Chapter 4
How to Keep Harmony in the Family
by Rose Phan 39

Chapter 5
How to Know the Truth
by Hugh Campbell 51

Chapter 6
People—The Solution That Was under Your Nose All Along
by Javier Guerrero 63

Chapter 7
Five Principles to Step into Your Leader Within
by Annette Fazio   73

Chapter 8
Change the World from the Front of the Room
by Tonya Hofmann   85

Chapter 9
Don't Just Survive, Thrive!
by Mari Muscio   95

Chapter 10
Create a Healthy Home, Energize Your Life, and
Change the World   103
by Bonnie Bradford

Chapter 11
Solving a Worldwide Epidemic
by Kim Dandurand   115

Chapter 12
How to Keep Your Pets Happy and Healthy
by Mary Stevenson   123

Final Note from Tracy Repchuk   133

Foreword

by Shawne Duperon
Nobel Peace Prize Nominee

At some point, you found your "mission" or your "purpose." For some of you, it was an easy find you claimed at a young age; for others, it evolved over time and actually delighted and surprised you. My delight and surprise evolved into a PhD in gossip of all things.

And here's the thing... When you find your mission (or it finds you) something exquisite happens. You start seeking ways to share it simply because you have to. You cannot NOT share it.

That's what happened with Project: Forgive, our case study for sharing good gossip. It's a leadership foundation that's reaching millions in social media and even garnered an endorsement from Archbishop Desmond Tutu.

The bonus for me was discovering that my mission of causing global forgiveness through good gossip is also woven into a bigger picture of many missions, including yours.

Consider that your mission is a piece to a global jigsaw puzzle of missions. Whether it's a passion for cleaner water, a focus on helping children of divorce, or even creating global forgiveness, your purpose is deliciously entwined with others who are committed to making a difference, too.

With that said, this book offers the actionable guidance you've been seeking. I don't just like Tracy Repchuk, I respect her. I respect her passion to be bold and forthright. I admire her courage to cause a difference rather than just talk about making a difference. If you're at that tipping point of causing, dive into this sage advice.

At some point, I believe, our missions may touch each other in some unusual way. It's exciting and comforting to know that we're in this causing together, sharing the same journey of daring to making a global impact and succeeding beyond our wildest expectations.

Dr. Shawne Duperon
Good Gossip Researcher, 6-Time EMMY® winner, Project: Forgive Founder

Chapter 1

Identifying Your Mission Critical Messages
by Tracy Repchuk

It's so interesting when I look back at my journey of where I came from and where I am today. How the messages I get, receive, follow, and give have become such a guiding light towards my ultimate destination.

I get interviewed for radio and TV a lot, and I'm often asked, "What is the driving factor to your success?" Have you ever been asked that question and figured out your answer? Here is why it's so interesting when I look back at my journey—the message has changed at key pivot points of my life.

I think this book needed to be written now because my message is so much bigger than me. I must admit when I started off at the age of nineteen after graduating college and starting my own software company, my answer was, "I want to make a million dollars."

I don't look back on that answer with disdain, but with a sense of pride for setting a goal and achieving it by the age of twenty-four. So every action I took was a successful step towards that. **My message back then was, "You have nothing to lose."** I was nineteen years old, starting the company in my parents' basement, and, except for a $25,000 loan to buy the equipment, I had nothing to lose by trying.

Once I had achieved that goal, I can see the next phase of my life was about growing and expanding the company. So my success factors were hard work, focus, and being adaptable to change. **My message became "To do whatever it takes."** I lived, eat, and breathed the company.

This realization introduced the common thread I could see throughout all my successful actions—advice given to me by a college business professor.

One day he pulled me aside two months before graduation and asked, "What are you going to do after you graduate?" "Go to Toronto and get a job as a programmer," was my immediate response. "Oh, no you're not," was his automatic reply. I looked puzzled wondering what fate I was about to be dealt. Then he said, "You're an entrepreneur. You're a natural born leader, you're dynamic, well liked, a great speaker, influencer, a genius, and an amazing problem solver." **The message for me was, "When the student is ready, the teacher will appear."**

I stood in wonder at his assessment of me, and of the possibility of not getting a job. My dad was a factory worker, and my mom stocked shelves. That wasn't even on my radar.

But here is the common thread of advice I apply to everything I do in business—which he said to me when I asked, "What kind of entrepreneur would I be?" The message he gave me was, **"All an entrepreneur needs to do is find the problem that needs to be solved and solve it."**

That piece of advice has made me liquid in my outlook, future seeking in my vision, and able to hold steady when required. In the volatile business of software development and technology, this was a vital skill to have. As hundreds of companies far greater than my own crumbled under the pressure of the dot com bubble burst and multiple recessions, for over thirty-one years now I have been an entrepreneur, never holding a job, having a boss, and being 100% responsible for my own success or failure.

And now I see the changes within become as fluid as water: how my success is driven by a season or place I am in my life and how, as that changes, so does my message and driving factors.

So the next phase of my life brought children. We had a staff of fifteen programmers, a big office and as soon as I became pregnant, the definition of success changed, along with my **message**, which was **"Actions speaker louder than words."**

What did that mean to me? We needed to make an incredibly bold, drastic, and revolutionary move in 1994 when both me and my husband decided to leave the comfort of our massive downtown office, put our children first, and revolve the company around our family dynamic. This meant sending our staff home to work virtually, and we set up a home office and a lifestyle that would leave our kids wondering why we never went to work.

We proved the new level of success in the realm of having it all. We raised three amazing kids, 24/7, on a sixteen-acre estate and twenty-two-room mansion nestled amongst woods and ponds, a playground where we held annual carnivals, skating rinks, and let them explore freely as children should, while we created the perfect working environment—twenty years before home office was a socially accepted response. Many said our actions were business suicide.

Some people talk about work life balance, having it all, harmony in the home, but we actually lived it. Which introduced the next message:

"Anything is possible, and creating your own reality is up to you."

Then the kids got older, and after giving them the best foundation we could imagine, we moved to the big city of Toronto and let them spread their wings and get a taste of the real world. They traveled on subways themselves at the age of twelve, added responsibility to their lives within the community, and joined organizations such as Youth for Human Rights and Drug Free Marshall's.

It was about then our next message arrived, and that came when my forty-year search for why are we here, what is my purpose, what am I supposed to be doing, those big bold life questions that many start to seek about now, could no longer be silenced. I had been searching since the age of three, and my next step was to hear: **"Freedom is actually a bigger game than power. Power is about what you can control. Freedom is about what you can unleash."** Harriet Rubin.

We went in search of spiritual and holistic answers, and moved from Toronto, Canada, to California for the next stage of our game. Starting from scratch, with no list, no leads, and no idea what I was going to do. It was early in my arrival to the USA that I discovered a man named Jim Rohn, whose message I had followed: **"If you are not willing to risk the unusual, you will have to settle for the ordinary."**

I reinvented and, in a few short months of my arrival, was on the internet marketing scene which was completely dominated by men—I had launched a book to #1 on Amazon, made six figures in my first six months, won New Internet Marketing Success of the Year from the World Internet Summit, and was flown all expenses paid from California to Singapore to appear in front of my very first audience of 3400 people.

This launched my speaking career beyond anything I could have dreamed of.

I catapulted to success in a way that was parallel to the

risk I took leaving my country, my business, my family and friends, bringing three young children to a new place, and starting from scratch in a place I had only read about in books.

I think if you take a look at your journey, you will have received Mission Critical Messages that became pivot points to your next level of success, as I can see has been the case with me.

And then, **you become the Mission Critical Message for someone else.**

So what information are you not getting out there? What skill have you hidden for fear, too big a risk, not ready to play your bigger game, uncertainty where to start, lack of confidence and the other false beliefs that prevent you from achieving the greatness you were sent here to deliver?

Everyone has a mission critical message for someone else.

I spent my first five years as an internet marketer traveling around the world, appearing on the world's largest stages in front of thousands, with the world's most amazing speakers— Jay Abraham, Jay Conrad Levinson, Mike Filsaime, Mark Joyner, Matt Bacak, Armand Morin, John Childers, Ted Nichols, Kevin Harrington, Loral Langemeier, Joel Comm, Robert Allen, the list is too big to continue. And after spreading my message that came from the subtitle of my book - **"You can Profit from Your Passions!"** I turned to television to reach millions.

My message for TV viewers was simple and revolved around **"Social Media Safety for Kids."** It wasn't my specialty but as a mom of three teens, and, as someone who was tech savvy and knew that only seven percent of parents were aware or even concerned about what their kids were doing online, and that over one million kids were affected by cyberbullying and cyberstalking on Facebook alone, it became a mission.

I hope by now you can see how my message is critical, and how yours is, too. Someone is waiting for you and your message.

So do you even know what your message is? My message to you for this question is to make sure you **have clarity on your message**. If you aren't clear, your prospect won't understand. If they don't understand, they won't buy. It's the key to your success for everything you do.

So what is my message now? What is my purpose now? Well, it's actually clear, and that is to get your message out to millions. I am the catalyst for messengers, CEOs, businesses, corporations, celebrities, game changers, and influencers. I use branding, online marketing, your website, positioning, and social media to help you reach your goals.

My purpose is to **"Help you reach millions with your message."**

Now ask yourself, "Is that something you would like help with?"

You see the world is at a tipping point. For the first time in history, we own the communication channel. Social media and the internet has leveled the playing field. Historically, major TV networks and newspaper empires (aka the government and other organizations controlling the message they want us to hear) held all the power, but that's no longer the case.

We can send a positive message to millions with a tweet. We can educate on good things that are happening in the world, put focus on organizations that are making a difference, expose global atrocities to mankind, promote positive leaders and influencers, and my biggest joy of all time right now—we can educate that you are a spiritual being, and with that comes the power to heal naturally.

My global personal message revolves around the desire to completely eliminate harmful drug companies and over the counter drug medications that damage man's ability to operate freely and enslaves him with side effects that far exceed the malady they were meant to correct and to promote holistic healers, practitioners, practices, and methods that are changing the world with education on your abilities and practices that can be applied for self health or spiritual healing.

These are the people I call game changers. Only 200 years ago you would have been hung for talking about the natural abilities you had that tapped into your spiritual awareness for healing and communication. But, today, there is a movement happening, and it's up to us to make sure it becomes the new standard of living.

We have a chance for the:
- preservation of humanity
- restoration of dignity and
- return of man to his natural spiritual abilities and awareness

So, if you have a message that you want to reach millions, then my last message to you today is to **get in touch with me**. Let me help you reach your goals, help you attain your success, craft your mission critical message so it's clear to the world, and create an online presence so you professionally match, rise above the competition, and reach millions with your message.

You are a messenger—with a mission critical message. Join the revolution.

So I hope you have gotten a broad overview of how to create an online presence where you professionally match, rise above the competition, and reach millions with your message.

I invite you to connect with me and let me help you.

If you would like me to guide or take your technology off your plate—do your online branding, website development, landing page, market funnel, logo, consult with you, be your partner, mastermind, then connect with me here to get familiar with my offerings.

www.FastActionResults.com

In addition, you will get more detail than I could give here from my Free Guide—How Your Brand, Websites and Social Media Work Together—once you opt-in.

I look forward to starting a relationship with you, finding out more about what you do, your vision, purpose, and mission so I can serve you in the deepest way possible.

I'll see you on the inside.

Tracy Repchuk
"Get Ready to Make an Instant Online Impact with a Fully Branded Complete End to End Website Presence and Message to Market System in Under 60 Days"

Find out more at: www.TracyRepchuk.com

Tracy media page - www.TracyRepchukMedia.com

Tracy speaker booking - www.TracyRepchukLive.com

Tracy Repchuk

Tracy Repchuk is an online marketing and social media strategist and speaker.

A seven-time international best selling author who has been an entrepreneur since 1985, she has helped thousands of clients get their message out around the world. She is also an internationally acclaimed speaker and motivator in over thirty-five countries. She keeps audiences engaged with her ability to break down complex concepts and turn them into formula based success.

Her first software business, which she started at the age of nineteen, still supports Fortune 100 companies. She has been nominated for awards such as Entrepreneur of the Year, Chamber of Commerce Business Woman of the Year, Coach of the Year and Stevie Awards for Business Mentor of the Year, received White House Presidential Award for Volunteer, State and Senate Awards, Provincial Volunteer and software development awards and has appeared in the International Who's Who in seven categories.

She graduated in Business Computer Systems and went on to receive a Certified Management Accountants designation. In 2007, Tracy won "New Internet Marketing Success of the Year" from the World Internet Summit and catapulted into success with her best selling book, speaking engagements, and extensive internet experience in web development, software integration, and marketing since 1994.

Tracy specializes in online marketing campaigns that build a cohesive corporate or personal brand using an integrated web strategy that helps you attract more leads, get more clients, and make more money. Her solutions are done with marketing and results in mind. In addition, she has appeared on TV: ABC, NBC, CBC, CTV, CBS, FOX, HGTV, 7 For Your Money, 4 On Your Side, WBZ, Report on Business Television, USA Today, Radio, magazine, newspaper and her work has appeared in over fifty publications including three motivational movies.

Chapter 2

The Health Crisis of the Youth— and the Solution
by Deanna Hansen

The last 16 years has been a journey of self-discovery. At the age of 30, I was thrown into an anxiety attack so bad I thought I was going to die. I was paralyzed with fear and didn't think I could breathe. But there was something more in store for me. In that moment of terror, I dove my hand into my abdomen, only to discover it was full of scar tissue. Having not had injury or surgery specific to the area, I hadn't realized this tissue state prior to this moment. Suddenly, I understood what stood in the way of my health.

As an athletic therapist since 1995, I always focused on deep tissue work. I was very aware of the texture of scar tissue but had never felt it in my own belly. I was fifty pounds overweight and seemed to store the majority of my size in my core. As a result, I never touched my abdomen because it brought up so much shame. I hated that place in my body and spent thousands of hours telling myself I was worthless and useless. All the efforts I made to change my appearance only caused more fat to accumulate and anxiety to build.

In that moment, however, when I dove my hand into my

belly, I understood why I would come home from a 5 mile run, dripping with sweat, only to find the area cold to the touch. This thick, dense tissue I was connecting with was blocking blood and oxygen flow.

The first night I explored the tissue for forty-five minutes. It was amazing how it relieved my anxiety immediately. I didn't want to stop. During the exploration, I had many insights. I couldn't help but sense I had tapped into something real, something profound. Somehow, I knew this would change my life.

The next day at work I was calm and excited to get back to the exploration. As soon as I came home, I lay on my back and once again began the journey of feeling my tissue. I felt lumps and it hurt, but I knew I was being guided by something outside of myself. After spending another period of time in this process, when I stood up, something had changed. I sensed I was taller, and my body felt lighter. When I went to the mirror, I was amazed at what I saw. I even started to cry. My belly looked flatter than it had looked in years. Only two days of this self-exploration and more positive things changed than years of hard work and struggle.

After two weeks of practicing this flowing form of deep tissue work, my chronic back pain improved, my bowel movements were flowing better, and the constant anxiety was dissipating. I flipped all of my patients onto their back and started working in their abdomen, only to find similar results.

This all began 16 years ago. Today, at the age of 46, I have transformed all aspects of my life and truly represent the bodywork practice I call Fluid Isometrics. In fact, I didn't develop Fluid Isometrics. It developed me. This work, on the most basic level, improves blood and energy flow to cells that have been previously blocked, thereby rejuvenating tissue, allowing for rapid healing of injury and providing better overall health for individuals.

The majority of people are simply surviving in their physical body, as the breath is shallow and comes from the wrong place. The practice of Fluid Isometrics changes the way we drive the body forward in time, by melting through the restrictions created from unconscious living and, consequently, breathing life into cells.

One of my passions is to reach the youth. They are the future, and I have to say, from a physical perspective, it's looking pretty dim. Their collapsed posture resulting from, in part, the age of technology, is causing them to strangle the diaphragm muscle, leaving them starving for oxygen.

We feed the body up to six hundred percent more oxygen when we use the diaphragm muscle to breathe compared to breathing with the muscles of the upper chest, as most do. Seventy percent of the oxygen receptor sites, called alveoli, reside at the base of the lungs. Shallow breathing simply won't pull the air in deeply enough to reach them. Waste removal is also limited, as we don't exhale fully or properly, leaving us toxic, and often swollen on a cellular level.

Today, many of the youth have aged rapidly from the accelerated internal collapse of the rib cage into the core, causing a displacement of organs and slowing of systems functioning. Digestion and elimination are compromised, causing individuals to be backed up with waste, and weight, and creating an environment ripe for disease. Their forward posture will have a direct effect on their emotional states as waves of emotion can't pass through tissue freely and their minds will be burdened with stress. As time goes on, there will be more of the youth developing more disease, and they will become a strain on the economy as a whole.

Of greatest concern is the fact that these young girls today, collapsing into their core at a rate so rapid we are seeing conditions such as a Dowager Hump, commonly an issue associated with the elderly, are the mothers of the future children. Their collapse leaves little room for healthy babies to grow and we are already seeing a dramatic increase in the number of babies with health challenges. This is everyone's problem. A world full of unhealthy people doesn't leave much hope for a high functioning world and planet.

There is a solution if we take action and decide to be responsible for our own health and healing. And it is simple if you follow the steps I have laid out in my programs.

It all comes down to space. There is a space/time continuum. As we age (go through time), we decrease in our internal space. We become shorter and wider. The majority of people would report that this is a true fact of aging. So in order to remove the time accumulated from the tissue, or age, we need to put the space back. This is what Fluid Isometrics does. It puts the space back into the tissue that time has taken away. Block Therapy is the self-care version of Fluid Isometrics and is simple to do, highly efficient, and teaches you to take care of yourself for life.

This is accomplished by understanding that scar tissue and collapsed fascia, both which block blood and oxygen flow, seal the tissue out of alignment with a force up to 2000lbs/square inch. This is an incredible force that gets its strength from its magnetic properties. Magnets, a far enough distance apart, have no effect on one another, but put them close enough, and they seal with a vengeance. Fluid Isometrics creates the space, and instruction and application of proper diaphragmatic breathing inflates the space. As oxygen is breathed into those newly created spaces gravity releases its hold on the tissue, creating a lightness and flow of energy to and from the area. This is healthy tissue, one that functions optimally as cells are fed and clean.

The third component of Fluid Isometrics is to own the space that has been created with proper postural habits. It isn't about doing a yoga class once a week, it is understanding that the way we use our body, all the time is what creates the signature posture that causes our suffering. With Fluid Isometrics you are shown how to create the space, inflate the space, and maintain the space. And once you have learned how to do it, it is at your fingertips for life.

I spent years developing Fluid Isometrics and researching the properties through real people getting real results. I then spent years developing Block Therapy to deliver this work in a simple program that anyone can do.

Fluid Isometrics is for everyone, because everyone is affected by gravity. The good news is that for every action there is an equal and opposite reaction. Gravity has a counterpart, the full conscious exhalation. Block Therapy teaches you how to access this incredible muscle and allows you to walk through time without your tissue accumulating pain, age, and disease. Even better, no matter where you are starting out with your health, Block Therapy takes time out of your tissue—it truly is the fountain of youth.

We have a choice in how we age. We can be a population that is thriving. It is up to us to lead the youth forward to a place of health and peace, not the struggle and disease that is present. We can do this together and with some simple understanding of how to create peace and harmony within, the world will only be a better place for us all.

Breathe & Believe

Deanna Hansen

In 2000, Deanna experienced a major breakthrough. Her large, heavy body stored much pain, and she felt weighed down and depressed. While experiencing the worst of a series of anxiety attacks, she intuitively pushed her hand into her abdomen and, at that moment, began a path of self-discovery.

In a short period of time, her body began to change. The weight was dropping, the chronic pain and issues were improving, and, most importantly, the depression and anxiety disappeared. She immediately began applying this to her existing patients, and the results were immediate and outstanding.

For fourteen more years, Deanna owned clinics where she practiced her new technique. In 2006, as word was spreading of the benefits of Fluid Isometrics™, she began teaching other therapists. It took time to create a language to transfer her wisdom she developed through her hands.

Now BlockTherapy is becoming a world-wide healing phenomenon. Find out for yourself.

Join the revolution. Get your free gift at:

www.UnBlockYourBody.com

Chapter 3

Write Your Story and Change the World
by Marci Baun

In 1999, I was browsing the web on my really slow modem connection, searching for good fiction to read. Imagine my shock when not one website came up. Oh, I found a few pages with stories, but none of them were edited, and most of them were painfully told. It made me really sad. You see, I'm an avid reader and have a deep love of the English language. Many of these stories had great potential, but there were so many typos, grammatical errors, and plot and character issues that the greatness of the story was hopelessly lost. The same was true for many of the non-fiction articles I came (and still come) across in my quest for good reading material.

I was discussing this with my then-roommate, and it hit us: we should pool our talents and resources and start an online magazine. We'd showcase short stories, poetry, non-fiction articles, photographic articles, interviews, and anything else that took our fancy. All of it would be subjected to rigorous editing. With my coding skills (I'd taken a few coding classes and designed a few websites prior to this) and our knowledge of the English language and writing, we'd create a place where people could come and read well edited, entertaining, and, sometimes, educational works.

Thus Wild Child Magazine was born, and it was a success. Within a few years, our efforts put us on of Writer's Digest's 101 Best Websites for Writers list.

Since that time, my roommate moved on, and the magazine grew into my two publishing houses. Our books have won awards, and we have continued to build on our reputation for excellence. I also discovered my passion extended beyond reading to include helping others attain that dream of being published. There is no greater satisfaction than in working with an author, helping them hone their writing skills, and polishing their "baby" into a piece that stays true to their vision and that they are proud to share with others.

As you can imagine, I meet a lot of people who have an idea for a book and would like some advice on how to get started—because, sometimes, starting a project is the hardest thing to do.

If you have a story to tell and don't know where to start, I'm excited to be able to share with you what I've been sharing with my authors, and others, for the past 16 years that I've been publishing. These steps are intuitive and applicable to just about any project you decide to tackle. Matter of fact, you might already do them, but just didn't see how they applied to writing that book.

Five paradoxically simple, yet complex, steps:

Step 1 — Choose the purpose and audience of your book.
Step 2 — Set a specific time to write.
Step 3 — Be kind to yourself.
Step 4 — Let it go and write.
Step 5 — Revise.

I say simple, yet complex, because the best laid intentions

can often be derailed. This is why step 1 is so important.

Step 1. Choose the purpose and audience of your book.

From memoir to self-help to fiction to other types of non-fiction, every author who writes a book has a reason to do it. For some authors, they have so many stories in their heads they have to write. There is no other option. For others, it's because they feel their story can uplift someone else. For others still, it's to educate. Without a purpose behind why you write, whether serious or not, you'll find it hard to do it.

So, be honest with yourself about why you're writing whatever you're writing. Is it to show others how to change their lives for the better? Is it because you've always wanted to be a bestselling author? Is it because you want to entertain people? Maybe you want to educate them on a topic you're passionate about.

All of these are valid reasons. They are. And it's very important that you don't make yourself wrong because your reason isn't what you deem "serious" enough. Why? Because, if you make the purpose of why you're writing the book wrong, you won't finish it. Remember, there's no such thing as a frivolous reason. Even entertainment has its place. Matter of fact, entertainment allows us to decompress and relax. It can make us smile, think, cry, or get angry. All of it has its place.

Because your purpose will be the driving force behind your dedication to keeping that appointment, sitting in that chair, and watching the words appear on the page as you write them, you have to be honest with yourself what it is.

Once you've established the purpose, you need to decide who your audience is. The language you'd use and how you'd write for a group of six graders isn't the same as the language you'd use and how you'd write for college students. By the same token, how you address college students differs from how you'd address business people in their 30s, 40s, and 50s. It even varies from sex to sex and generation to generation.

Long before I became a publisher, I was a chautauqua performer in schools. (A chautauqua performer is someone who portrays historical characters.) My very first performance was to a group of approximately 300 third to sixth graders. Up to that point, all of my writing experience had been focused on essays. I'd taken one storytelling class, but, for some reason, I didn't think of using those skills.

I wish I had.

Children of this age don't want to be lectured at, which is essentially what I was doing. They want to be entertained. It didn't matter that I was dressed in period clothing, or that I said I was Lola Montes. I was boring. The entire performance was boring, and the audience let me know. They booed. It was a humbling experience I've never forgotten. It also taught me a valuable lesson.

If you want to reach your audience, you've got to know who they are.

So, sit down and figure out your purpose and your audience.

Step 2. Set a specific time to write.

Let's face it, we're bombarded with demands on our time every single day. When writing isn't our job, it's hard to make time for it. But, if you really want to finish that novel/memoir/non-fiction how-to/self-help book, you've got to set a time to write. Whether this is an hour a day, an hour every other day, or even a few hours once a week, this time has to be set in stone. You don't do anything else—barring emergencies, illness, or death, that is—but write.

Trust me, if you don't literally put this into your calendar, the likelihood of you consistently sitting down to write is slim to none. This is what professional authors do. Most people will always find something else "more important" to do. And you'll have to make sure your loved ones know that at "such and such time, I will be writing. Please don't disturb me." It might take a few times for them to see that you're serious and truly mean it, but you can do it.

There will be days where the words flow from you like ink from a pen. Conversely, there will be days when you're sure the story goblin came and stole all of your ideas. Even on those days, when it seems like you can't write a logical sentence, write anyway. You are building that muscle and honoring that part of you that has declared it must be heard.

It's on those days, in particular, you'll need to be kind to yourself.

Which brings me to step 3.

Step 3. Be kind to yourself.

If you don't put the inner critic on the shelf before you begin, you'll be done before you start. Every idea, every genre you consider will be shot down in a spectacular ball of flames.

That critic can be very helpful, but, more often than not, it stops forward motion. Those days when you've hit the wall with ideas and writing (aka writer's block) are the days your critic is playing hardball. If you recognize what's happening, you'll be able to silence it and you'll see the word count climb. If you aren't able to, for whatever reason, have patience. Keep writing. Write goals, write a haiku about your critic, or even begin your sessions with "I don't know what to write" and let it go from there. There may be several more sentences following it in the same vein. That's okay. It happens to everyone, even veteran authors.

Whatever you do, just write because some days are just like that.

Allowing yourself to have those days will ensure that other days will be productive. And, sometimes, when you aren't sure what to write and you see everything you've put on paper so far is dross, you'll come across the most brilliant sentence, or astoundingly deep idea that you'll marvel at how you were the one who created something so beautiful.

But it all starts with being kind. You have to allow yourself to make those "mistakes" and not hold out for perfection. Perfection is an illusion that only keeps you stuck.

Once you've put your critic on the shelf, you can move on to step 4.

Step 4. Let it flow and write.

Now that you've set a time for yourself to write, determined to be kind to yourself, and chosen the purpose of why you are writing, it's time to jump in feet first and write.

Recognize your first draft will be rough. You might have notes in places telling yourself to research this a bit more or perhaps to look for another word because the one you have just doesn't work. Don't worry about it. Know that you're going to be coming back to it, and you'll fix it then. The important thing at this moment is to get your thoughts and ideas into tangible form.

You could write the first draft in a month, or it could take you several months, depending on how long you determine the book needs to be. You may not even know how long it's going to be until it's done. The length of time and the number of words aren't that important that first draft. I know authors whose first draft are over 100,000 words, but after they revise, it's now only 70,000.

If it helps you write, you can give yourself a deadline, or aim for a certain word count each week/session. If you do set a deadline or word count goals, be sure to them realistic as you'll be more apt to continue. And you won't know what your output can be until you start writing. Some authors who can pound out 10,000 words in one sitting; others are happy if they add 200 words a day. As long as you continue to see that word count rise, don't worry about it too much. Stay focused and keep your eye on the prize.

Once you've written your first draft, this is when you are ready to start step 5.

Step 5. Revise.

Recognize that it's probably going to be very rough. Every veteran author knows this. They know whatever they write will need revising, some TLC, and time. That's right. Time. Let that first draft sit for at least a week. (I know authors who'll let things sit for at least a month before reviewing it again.) They don't send it off to a friend for their opinion or read it again just to review it. They just let it sit.

This is important because it gives you distance from what you've just written. When you return, it'll be easier to spot any typos, missing/extra words, plot holes, syntax errors, pace problems, flow problems, etc.

After that week has passed, open up the file and, with your critic on the shelf, read through it. Read through it as if it's not yours and with an open mind. Read it aloud. Anything your tongue trips over needs to be rewritten. It might be something as simple as changing one word. It might require rewriting a sentence or an entire passage. Whatever needs to be done, do it objectively. Self-flagellation isn't allowed whenever you're creating *anything*. It's counterproductive and destructive. So, keep those whips in the closet. This is not the time to use them.

I'm going to repeat that objectivity is key here. This is what the professionals do. They know that in order to create a masterpiece, they'll have to pull it apart and put it back together again maybe several times. They look for the good and the bad without judging themselves as wrong when they find mistakes.

So, while you're reading, look for what's working and what isn't. Be prepared to cut where needed, even if it's something you love. When I wrote this chapter for this book, I had a sentence that I thought was really fantastic, but it stopped the flow. No matter how much I massaged it, I got stuck and couldn't move forward. As much as I hated doing it, I cut it.

As author Sir Arthur Quiller-Couch said, be willing to "murder your darlings."

Besides, there's nothing to say you can't save it and use it elsewhere. Just copy and paste it into a new file. You never know, that sentence/description/section just might work perfectly in another book.

So, get to it. It's time for you to listen to that little voice whispering inside of you, urging you to share your talents with others.

Marci Baun

"Self-Publishing with an Expert"

Are you an entrepreneur looking to establish your expertise in your field?

Are you certain your knowledge can improve someone else's life, but are paralyzed with doubt about where to start? Have you completely given up on writing that book that could change someone's life?

There's a lot to publishing and it can be overwhelming.

Let me help you. I'd like to give you a free copy of my guide **"5 Steps to Finally Getting Published without Breaking the Bank"**. In it you'll find:

- The five simple steps to prepare your book for publishing on a budget
- How to set up your content so it's easy to get done
- What readers are looking for so you have hungry buyers
- The critical factor that can't be skipped
- What your book needs to really be successful

Head to: www.FinallyPublished.com

See you in print!
Marci

Marci Baun

Born and raised in California, Marci Baun fell in love with the English language in the third grade when she discovered the *Little House on the Prairie* series. She quickly developed a voracious appetite for books. Her desire to be a published author started in the sixth grade after reading a short story that inspired her to write *her* first story.

She discovered she could explore the world, and beyond, before she was old enough to travel on her own. This allowed her to expand her knowledge of history, other cultures and countries, nature, and science and instilled a desire to learn more about the world around her.

This desire drove her to excel in college where she studied vocal performance and business for her bachelor degree, graduating *magna cum laude* from the University of the Pacific, and, later, vocal performance for her master degree, graduating *summa cum laude*.

The owner of two award-winning, publishing houses, she has spent the last 16 years dedicating herself to publishing high-quality fiction and non-fiction works.

Her interest in history, music, opera, theater, swimming, cycling, nature, travel, and writing have led her on numerous adventures around the world, eventually bringing her to Los Angeles, where she now resides with her husband and daughter.

Follow Marci at:
Website: http://www.marcibaun.com/
Facebook: http://www.facebook.com/marcibaun
Twitter: http://www.twitter.com/marcibaun
Blab: http://www.blab.im/marcibaun

Chapter 4

How to Keep Harmony in a Family?
by Rose Phan

Harmony in a family brings peace and happiness so that we can pursue our goals without interrupted disturbance. Success can be achieved easier with less emotional roadblocks. So, how can we keep harmony in our family?

There are five major steps to keep harmony in a family.

1. Order
2. Respect
3. Communication
4. Empathy
5. Caring

Before clarifying the formula, I'd like to share with you how I have lived and how I developed my formula.

I've lived the best and the worst of both the Eastern and the Western lifestyles. I went to a private French Catholic school in South Vietnam and was influenced by Vietnamese and Chinese cultures and philosophies and a mix of liberal cultures in the U.S.

After the fall of Saigon in April 1975, I moved to California and have lived in the United States for 39 years.

I didn't escape communist Vietnam until a year after the fall of South Vietnam. In a quest for freedom, we risked our lives in the ocean with badly equipped small wooden boats. It was our main choice to keep our family together: parents, five children and our great grandmother, along with other families.

We valued the family unit and chose to live or die together, away from communism. It was a journey of miracles. From the time of leaving in secret by a small river, to the canal of Cap St. Jacques, we finally decided to continue our escape with our boats even without enough water or gasoline because the prearranged larger boats did not show up at our rendezvous time. After a few days at sea, our boats ran out of water, but we got our first miracle: a huge storm. Then, the next day, we ran out of gasoline and were captured by a communist patrol ship.

On the way back to Vietnam, I knew that my father would be executed because he was the leader of this quest. And our family surely would be broken apart because we would be sent to a labor concentration camp. No more family unit that we valued so much.

A second major miracle happened: my father and a few brave men took over that ship and carried on to Thailand, along with three wounded among our people.

That was a fight for survival, and to keep our family together. I knew then that my life was for a purpose and a meaning: to be worthy of so many sacrifices and most of all, for the miracles that led to my survival.

Arriving in California on August 2, 1976, my family was in a completely different world, with a different language and culture. We still tried to make our living by working and helping each other in every way we could. We endured hardships, we appreciated our new beginning by learning the new language, going to school, working long hours and chipping in what we made into the family bucket, so we could grow and live the best way possible. With our united way of living, we honored our elders with respect and love, and we supported each other along the way.

When it came time to marry and have my own family, I got married in 1984 to a man who chased patiently after me for five years. As of business, in partnership with my husband, I won multiple awards, such as Entrepreneur of the Year, Pioneering Women and Business Woman of the Year, and was featured in many major business publications, such as Working Women Business Magazine, Reader's Digest, the Los Angeles Times, the Orange County Register, International Trade Magazine and others.

Here are the elements of the formula:

Step 1. Order

I decided that there must be order in everything, either in family or business, private or public, in order to keep peace and balance. I have consciously chosen to prioritize my spouse as number one on the list before having kids, and also after having kids. It is natural for most women who become mothers to switch most or all attention to their children and to neglect their spouse in many ways. Most women forget that their husband can be considered their oldest baby who always needs security and reassurance of their affection and attention.

So, I had made that decision from the start that I would put my husband as the most important person to me after God. This might sound standard or normal to most of you, but to many cultures, most women still make this common mistake and wonder why their man seems to drift away. I expected the same from my husband and constantly reminded him that I wanted and needed to be his number one.

With that in mind, I choose to fulfill his needs sexually and emotionally, without forgetting to honor and fulfill my own needs. Without knowing how to love yourself, it may be hard to know how to love others.

Step 2. Respect

Respect your differences as a man and a woman. In 1999, my husband and I got involved in a marriage and family enrichment program. We are continuously learning and reminding ourselves to work on our relationship and our family. We read and attended retreats, listened to experts, and developed our own adjustments. We learned to respect each other's differences and give each other space when it is needed. It is so completely different between a woman who usually wants to talk it out or let it out immediately and a man who usually may just go into a cave to find a solution until he is ready to come out to solve it. This opposite character alone can cause great dissatisfaction if we do not understand and respect and wait for the right time. So, respect is to accept our differences and to give each other the necessary space.

Step 3. Communication

We all know this can be the most difficult and challenging requirement. It takes two to communicate, but listening is the most important. Knowing how to listen is something we cannot take for granted. With our busy daily lives, especially after having children, our load of responsibilities gets heavier. Couples tend to always be in a hurry and hardly have time to sit down face to face, eyes to eyes. Remember element No. 1 above: our priority is our spouse. We make time to resolve any disagreement or conflict by sitting down to talk and to listen. Listen and repeat what we hear to prevent any misunderstandings. This sounds simple but it takes real effort to pay attention to each other's feelings and thoughts. Just listen with respect and love and take time out when tempers start to rise. We promise each other that no matter how angry we may be for any reason neither of us will leave the house. We may go to the backyard or to the garden but we do not physically leave the house in anger. Most of all, self-control to not spit out any degrading or nasty words when one is angry is worth the effort.

Step 4. Empathy

"Do to others what you want to be done unto you." How many times do we feel that we are right and the other is wrong without any further consideration? For sure, that was the harsh word from the other party that we heard with our own ears. It might offend and hurt us so badly that we can no longer be understanding or forgiving. However, I always remember that I cannot let my relationship and my family be torn apart because of just words, no matter how negative the words might sound to my ears. I have to remember that because of the sensitive nature of being a woman, and the shortcoming character of being a man, the words especially in the heat of the moment should not be carried in a woman's heart with resentment or judgment. Instead, think of the possibility of misunderstanding and empathize with your spouse's reaction and be gentle, showing support and understanding. Especially when a spouse has encountered a failure in business or any emotional struggle, the other spouse should learn to empathize with the other person's pain and hardship. To empathize is to put you in the other person's shoes and to understand and to forgive. To empathize is to understand without judgment.

Step 5. Caring

This is one of the elements of the heart. We care because we want to pay attention to the other person. It takes work and effort to show that we care, not only by our words, but through our attitude and our actions. Most mornings, I make a healthy smoothie for each of my family members. It's a cup of complete nutrition for breakfast that starts everyone with the right energy for the day. Quick, healthy, and full of caring, it shows my husband and three sons that I care. I know each of them works very hard in their business and never expects much from me. As a wife and a mother, I care for each of them tremendously. I feel compassion for their hard work and their mission in life.

So, in order to keep harmony in a family, there must be love, which should include, in order of priority: respect for space, communication for listening, empathy for understanding, and caring for compassion.

The family that practices these five major elements should concentrate on love, which keeps harmony naturally. It may be challenging sometimes because of our differences, but I usually act as the queen of my family and set a routine of eating dinner together, nightly praying together, Sunday church together, activities such as hiking, camping, picnicking, and celebrating together. This became less frequent when our children had adapted to different schedules, but the principle is still there. So far, we have gotten together to share our joy, our challenges, either in business or in personal life, our disagreements, or our experiences. We make time for family discussions and updates and even to sort out our roadblocks. We usually resolve our issues with our brains and hearts together.

One of the most recent significant arguments between my husband and me over how I reacted to a social matter caused extreme tension. I resented him wanting to change my personality to fit his expectations. I am an Asian woman and very conservative, but I appear more liberal because I've adopted the Western freedom of speech. This directness may fit with the American people but it can easily backfire in the Asian community. I usually get in trouble for being straightforward and direct, even though it does no harm to anybody. My husband is the opposite. He is tender and less vocal. So, you can imagine we clash frequently.

We called a meeting with our three boys to discuss our latest issue. They asked questions, they listened, and they shared their viewpoints. They spoke respectfully but honestly. We listened and took them seriously. The next morning, we spoke separately to figure out a solution. This talk helped us recognize our weaknesses and our strengths. We came to an agreement, and I willingly chose to make an adjustment. Our anger or resentment towards each other was resolved, and we were at peace and harmony with our choices. That took humility and respect between parents, and between children and spouses.

We were so happy that we didn't give up on our relationship because of frustration or resentment, or feeling misunderstood or unappreciated. We cared enough to take the time to share, to communicate, to understand, to empathize, and, most of all, to love so that we could keep the peace and harmony during our many more years together. Remember, when a couple is having any conflict, it usually is important to have an objective qualified third person with a set of sharp ears, a positive brain, and godly heart to help you clear your blindness and roadblock. When we're in conflict, it's hard to resolve our problems ourselves. It would be wise to have the right counselor to help.

It is definitely harder to work out things than to give up, but keeping a family in harmony is worth all the hard work and effort. We cannot be selfish and irresponsible by taking the easy way out. We must think of the domino effect when we make the wrong decision and things get tough or don't go the way we expect. The sun always shines after the storm, but if we still have a roof over our heads to keep the family together after the storm, that is what matters. Keeping harmony in a family is an art and we do it so the following generations can have faith that family life is worth living.

I am so blessed to have lived the best of both worlds and among many cultures. I have always found solutions to any challenge, both family and business. I have been a family counselor for seventeen years and I would be glad to be of help to you. Please check out www.RosePhan.com for more assistance.

We, as a family, always remember to say a prayer to thank

God for our blessings and for our challenges because we believe that God is our true protector and lover in everything we do and live for.

I hope that my simple formula can help you keep your family harmonious and keep the love of God as the real priority.

Rose Phan
Speaker - Image Consultant - Life Coach

What's Next?

Do you feel suffocated with your relationship? Do you feel sad, depressed or stressed out with your teenagers' challenges? Do you suffer from the conflict between your in-laws and your spouse? Do you feel like you've hit a dead-end in your life? Do you feel unappreciated or criticized? Do you keep having the same stupid fights? Do you want to be truly happy?

Do you know that couples, who can learn to solve problems constructively together, cut their risk for stress related health problems including depression, cardiovascular disease, lowered immunity and even cancer?

Do you know that you can take the initiate to make a difference for a better life, better health? Do you want to get your life, your relationships, and your family back to balance and harmony?

Learn how to detect your inner causes and to resolve outer problems. Rose can help you help yourself to live to the fullest.

For more details, you can visit:

Website: http://www.RosePhan.com
Facebook: http://www.facebook.com/rphan11
Twitter: http://www.twitter.com/rphan1 (@rphan1)
Linkedin: http://www.linkedin.com/pub/rose-phan

Rose Phan

In 1976, Rose Phan survived a near-death experience escaping to freedom from Vietnam. She began a new life in California as a piano teacher, a certified court interpreter, and a successful entrepreneur. Rose and her husband started a computer business in 1989, won a government contract to upgrade computers at low cost, then developed remote video surveillance technology. She received multiple business awards, such as Entrepreneur of the Year, Pioneering Women and Business Woman of the Year, and was featured in many major business publications, such as Working Women, Business Magazine, Reader's Digest, the Los Angeles Times, the Orange County Register, International Trade Magazine and others.

She and her husband have worked well in business and continue to grow harmoniously with their three mature sons in Laguna Hills, California. They celebrated their 31st wedding anniversary in April 2015.

In 2014, the Phans and their three sons created BellaVieNetwork.com an online shopping network designed to fund community-based charities. Members can purchase with a purpose at their convenience while earning and saving, helping themselves and others in order to save time, to earn extra money and to enjoy a beautiful life. They've also started a sister site, BeVieWellness.com, a heartfelt creation born of a genuine dream to enhance the wellness of people's lives.

Chapter 5

How to Know the Truth
by Hugh Campbell

Life on this planet is changing faster than most people realize. It used to be that everyone could put these changes at arm's length but no longer! We are all part of something much bigger than our personalities, affiliations, and, for that matter, much of what we have ever learned. Some have suspected that there is more to life than we knew, and I am here to reveal to you something that will change your life and open the door to the "more". We are on the verge of one of the greatest shifts in human consciousness that has ever been witnessed. This shift will change all the rules on this planet, and either people will evolve to become a part of this change or they will literally be checking out of this life. The explanation for all of this would take longer than I have time available, so I ask you to take a leap of faith and give me a few pages to make my point.

Life has been all about finding balance in our personal lives, business, and spiritually. In reality, when we become spiritually centered, everything else falls into place. That is how we become successful, and this aspect of being spiritually centered is becoming the focus of our lives. This is an energetic shift, a spiritual evolution, a new stage in our development. There have been other stages in the development of humanity, and each new progressive wave has moved new people into positions of influence and others out. So who can you turn to that you can trust to help guide you? The answer will surprise you because it is YOU! It has always been you, but it is the part of you that goes beyond the limitations of your physical mind. It is from the part of you that is connected to All That Is. This may sound quite absurd, but it's the truth. As C.W. Leadbeater, the person that was responsible for bringing the secrets of Eastern philosophy to the West in the early 1900's, said, *"It is one of the commonest of mistakes to consider that the limit of our power of perception is also the limit of all there is to perceive."*

The way we impact everything around us begins with our perceptions. Many don't think about where their perceptions came from or how they affect our lives. Yet our perceptions and what we hold in our consciousness is the most important part of us. They are what we transmit out into the world and what we attract to us. We may not believe that we're doing anything at all, but what we are missing is the key principal:

Everything is energy.

Many of us have heard this before, but very few truly understand that in fact energy is "all" there is. This becomes especially significant when it comes to our thoughts. Our thoughts are energy, and we hold these energetic thought forms within our energetic field. All energy has a vibration to it so it not only influences our vibrational frequency, but it becomes part of what is sent out from us and what is attracted to us. Our vibrational frequency attracts people and experiences that are of similar vibration. Do you remember growing up and, as you changed, the people and experiences changed, too? If we want to increase our impact in changing this world, we need to understand the concept of the pebble in the pond. A pebble dropped into a pond will send ripples to every corner of the pond. This is the true energetic image of our place and interaction in this world. We are already connected to everything so all we need to do is look at what we hold in consciousness and how that affects what we want. We are creating the interaction to everything around us based upon our energetic vibration. Gandhi once said, *"You must be the change you want to see in the world."*

    The key has always been with us. Once we know what to change in us, we automatically become the change around us. I know this sounds very un-business like, but I can tell you that what I learned with my MBA does not compare with what you are about to learn.

    There is an aspect of us that has always been explained in very vague terms, and it is called our higher-self. We all have a higher-self that we can connect to and get the answers we need, but many people aren't aware that there is such a thing, nor are they aware there is a simple to learn tool that can be used to connect to it. I call this method of asking and receiving answers Resonant Testing™ because in energetic terms you are connecting with answers that resonate with you.

    When I discovered this technique, my engineering mind wanted to understand how this worked. I can now explain it based upon years of using Resonant Testing™ and also having uncovered the spiritual principles upon which it is based. Resonant Testing™ gives you yes or no answers that you pose to your higher-self. You literally are connected to this source and the answers that you receive can be trusted. In today's world, how often do you know what the truth of a situation is when you're entering into a new business or personal relationship? What if you could test these relationships and ask probing questions and know the truth? To me, this has been a game changer and is what I believe is the most important message and tool that I can convey.

I have taught hundreds of people to use this technique, and I can assure you that 90% of the people pick it up very quickly. Many people will jump to the conclusion that this is muscle testing or kinesiology, but it is important to make this distinction. In these other methods, there is not an intention to connect to your higher-self. There is a belief that your muscles are literally giving you the answers. This is akin to saying your speech is created or originated by the muscles in your jaw. Intention is a very important aspect of our lives. Connecting to your higher-self and getting answers does not originate in the muscles. When you understand this distinction, you understand the power you have at your fingertips.

The other important aspect of using this tool is what happens over time. How many of us were pre-warned with a gut feeling that we wished we had listened to? That was your intuition trying to steer you away from a situation. Intuition is only one feature of the connection to your higher-self. The more Resonant Testing™ you do, the stronger that connection becomes and the more intuition, guidance, and insight you will receive. You'll see things change in your life, and you'll feel the difference.

There is one caveat I should mention: as you use this tool, the channel to your higher-self expands. You become more aware and in tune with what is for your highest good. You'll notice your behavior will also change. You're essentially allowing more divine energy to flow into your life, and I can say from personal experience that my life has become magical.

Before I show you how to get the answers you want, I need to give you a little instruction first. Resonant Testing™ gives you answers to "yes" or "no" questions. In order to get a clear and strong answer, your questions cannot be vague. Rephrase the question if you have any doubts. Ask several ways if necessary to be sure.

Stand with your feet shoulder width apart and place your hands together in front of your heart as shown in Figure 1.

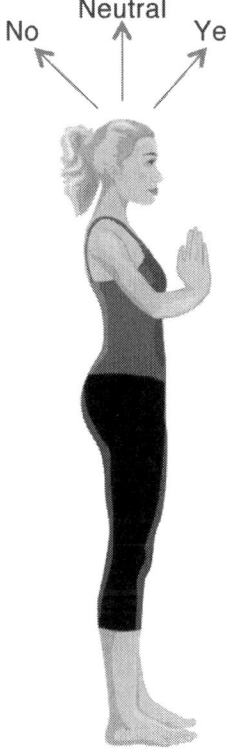

Figure 1

Resonant Testing™ is a two-part process. You ask your question, then quiet your mind and let your body move to give you the answer. If you try to control how your body moves, you won't get an accurate response. Since strong will about an outcome *can* influence the answer, you must relax and empty your mind. When you body moves forward, this is a "yes". If it moves backward, it's a "no". There is also a neutral position if something is neither good nor bad for you. If you start going in a circular motion, you are either fighting the answer, trying to control the outcome of an answer or trying too hard to understand what is happening. Just release your control and let your body move on its own.

For your first question, ask, "Is my name (*say your name*)?" For most people, they will lean forward, unless you used a nickname. Your real name is what you came into this world with, and it is part of your vibration. This is another little secret that most people don't know: *you chose your name before you incarnated and your parents only sponsored you into this realm*. People that don't use their real name are working at a disadvantage because they're not getting the full energetic value that comes from their real name. If you lean backwards when asking about your name, then it is possible your testing will be reversed from normal. If your testing is reversed, you will lean backward for yes and forward for no (*very rare but it happens*).

Testing for food or health care products.
Simply ask, "Is it good for me?" If something tests neutral, check a different brand. Why buy something that tests bad or neutral?

Testing quantities such as for supplements.
After you have tested whether a supplement is good for you, ask, "How many of these should I take today?" Then start counting slowly, 1,2,3. If you lean forward on three, that is the cut off number, so take two supplements.

There are no limits to what you can test. Your spirit guides know what you need and will help you get the answers when appropriate. It is always about alignment and what is right for you at the time.

Things that you may not get answers to.
The first thing that most people want to know (including myself) was whether you can get winning lotto numbers. This was an interesting process for me. I tested on lottery numbers and actually got a set of numbers to play. I went and played them and didn't win a dime. I discovered that, in some instances, your higher-self will let you play something out for the lesson involved. What my guides told me later is that money is energy, and most people aren't able to handle that much energy coming into their lives. Think about the lives of many lotto winners. My higher-self allowed me to go forward so that I would learn this lesson about the effects of coming into a large amount of money.

You will not get answers for things that have to do with free will. Free will is an important aspect of our life experience. When you ask things like, "should I marry this person" or "should I take this job", you'll generally get a neutral response. There is a way to work around this. If you ask if a person or job is energetically compatible with you, this will help you make your decisions and give you the answer you're seeking. This is a real breakthrough question and is an example of how to be creative with your questions!

I mentioned in the beginning that I was led to how all this works. Why standing up, why have your hands in front of your heart? What is really happening here? When you look at a person with their hands in front of their heart, the first thing that comes to mind is that they are praying. I believe this is essentially what is happening, but what I am outlining is all the aspects of what makes it really work. There is a reason, and it gets pretty interesting. When we are in spirit form, we are connected to all of life. When we come to this plane of existence, we are separated from all that is. The instrument that facilitates this separation is the mind. The mind, and its main instrument the ego, is the veil that keeps us from connecting from all that is. If the mind didn't facilitate this separation, we wouldn't be able to have this separate experience nor would we even wish to trudge through the daily mundane and drama of this existence. It'd be like someone telling you the ending of a book before you read it. Why would you want to read it?

We're all here to experience this life and learn from it. As you know, human history hasn't had a lot of people that were connected to the Source of All That Is. That's also the reason the understanding of how this tool works hasn't been in wide use until now.

By standing up during the process, the message is clearer because the full length of your body will move. You may remember references in the Bible of "and the spirit moved him." Putting your hands over your heart with your fingers pointing up taps into the heart and crown chakras.

The heart chakra has twelve petals, as shown in the picture below from C.W. Leadbeater's book *The Chakras: A Monograph* from around 1927.

If you look closely at the crown chakra, you will see that

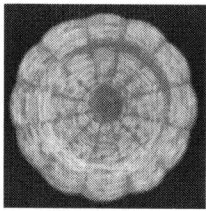

the very center of the crown chakra has an exact replica of the heart chakra!

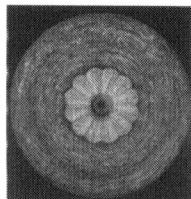

When you place your hands in front of your heart, you create an energetic pathway from your heart chakra to your crown chakra. This pathway bypasses the mind and connects to your higher-self. You're bypassing the limitations of your mind and of this world and connecting to All That Is. When you stop to think about this, you realize that nothing in your life will ever be the same. You will know things that are not only for your highest good but for the good of others also. This is one tool that will change the world, and now you know how to use it.

I believe the reason this tool is now being made available is because it's time to wake up from the lives humanity has led in the past. We're at a new stage in our evolution. Buddha taught the sacredness of life, Jesus taught the brotherhood of man, and now it's time for loving allowance. It's time to understand that all of us are One and each of us is on a path that is perfect for us. I believe that all of us who are on this planet today are here to play an important part in the evolution of humanity. This tool will be a part of opening the doors to that evolution.

Many years have passed since I started testing. It has opened me up to all of life and has created a connection which has allowed me to have conversations with plants, animals, and my spirit guide Xenanthium. I have channeled writings from Xenanthium for several years, which are currently being published by several spiritual magazines and online journals.

Blessings to all!

Hugh Campbell

Healing Body Spirit Mind

Hugh's Special Offer

He can be booked for individual or group classes, lectures, and healings. He can be contacted at:

Hugh@HealingBodySpiritMind.com
www.HealingBodySpiritMind.com
(714) 782-7596

Contact Hugh for a free monthly subscription to Healing News! A channeled writing from Xenanthanium is in each issue. Back issues are on the website!

Hugh Campbell

Hugh Campbell spent over thirty years in engineering. Starting at Xerox Corporation in the late 70's, he worked on the first optical input scanner and other research and development projects. He's spent the last thirteen years of his career as an aerospace engineer for such companies as Rockwell, Boeing, and DRS, developing unique solutions to complex engineering problems.

Hugh has researched alternative energy longer than he has been in engineering. Through the works of Nikola Tesla and other writings, Hugh found a whole new energetic way of looking at everything in the universe. The more this area was investigated, the more it opened doors to alternative thinking, especially in the areas of science, medicine, and healing. A friend introduced Hugh to the healing power of herbs and then he discovered homeopathic remedies, essential oils, Bach Flowers and then Pranic and Crystal healing.

Hugh put the same research principles used as an engineer to investigate what appeared to be in complete opposition to everything he knew. In his studies, he found that, when the proper scientific explanations were applied, metaphysics and science were two different sides to the same coin. As part of this journey, a shaman introduced Hugh to his spirit guide Xenanthium, an energetic being that creates galaxies. Through these writings, the secrets of galaxies and of the universe itself were revealed. Hugh has been channeling writings from Xenanthium for many years and is working to complete a book of these writings.

Hugh has incorporated many different healing modalities

together to help clients heal on the spiritual, emotional, and physical levels. He uses life and soul coaching, Pranic Healing, Crystal Healing, healing perfumes, Chakra Healing Plates, and more. He is also a teacher of Resonant Testing™ and other spiritual tools.

Chapter 6

People – The Solution That Was under Your Nose All Along
by Javier Guerrero

I will never forget that cool evening in Ecuador in 1988. I discovered that a person can be naturally happy—simply as a spiritual being. This realization hit me at a most tumultuous time, when I seemed to have lost control of the helm of my life. And it happened while doing a communication exercise on a course that was so entirely new to me that I hardly knew how I'd wound up there.

Furthermore, that same technique was from a body of knowledge that could be applied to the individual, his family, groups, nations, and the planet, as all these were composed of individuals, spiritual beings themselves. Now, this seemed the kind of activity that would enable me to effectively help others and society. That excited me, as it was precisely what I was looking for!

From that point, I decided to study this subject and begin to apply it. It didn't even matter if it meant that I would have to leave the city and country where I was born and raised, possibly for the rest of my life. And that is exactly what happened. I just knew it was my duty.

One of the aspects that intrigued me the most was that I could help entrepreneurs, businessmen, organizations, and groups of any size manifest their purpose by making them more efficient and organized just by caring for the individuals within them. Why? Because the individuals *are* the foundations of these groups. This is how I became a comprehensive business consultant.

Years later, after having completed the highest training available on the subject as a master consultant, I've had the honor of successfully helping individuals and companies, small and large, attain their missions in higher quality and volume while maintaining a happy and productive personnel.

In the course of my career of doing this, managing employees was the main barrier I've encountered among my clients. Finding, hiring, training, and retaining optimum employees or associates that really helped in the endeavors of the companies was the biggest challenge. So much so that some considered throwing in the towel and finding an alternative solution—like becoming employees themselves again to avoid all the "hassles". All these years of helping clients conquer this aspect of management made for a learning experience for me as well as for my clients. I've decided to share this learning and summarize it for you.

It has often been said that the human resource is the most important resource you have. However, with the advent of the tech age we live in, it's been getting harder and harder to justify such a datum.

There's a growing tendency among professionals of many different walks of life to forego most staffing needs with a good computer system. Executives start operating solo or with a minimal crew, downsizing their offices while continuing to service their clients with as little "human-touch" as possible.

This phenomenon is not exclusive to the private professional operations, either. It's not uncommon to hear that big monster companies and even government entities have downsized their staff element and substituted their human resource with cyber-power.

On casual inspection, this seems to make sense. But if genuinely workable, please answer these questions: Why do economies seem to be generally declining? Why are local and even national governments in financial trouble and resorting to taxing the people they govern even more to survive? If downsizing manpower saves money, then why do groups seemingly struggle more financially?

When you substitute a person's function for a computer capable of doing that function, what are you missing? Is it competence? It would seem the computer can do many functions faster and with fewer errors than most people can. Is it personal problems? We know it is hard on executives when staff let that affect their work! Is it breathing and having to take meal breaks? Another thing you were hoping to get rid of when it comes to ideal staff. So, what's that vital quality we're missing here?

Well, there's one major difference between the man-operated function and the computer-operated one that may have been overlooked. That quality—uninspected and shrouded behind most executives' inability to handle—was: WILLINGNESS! This is what the best computer in the world doesn't have. It's the single quality that has been lost and what so many companies and governments haven't been able to replace in their automation of so many functions.

You may say, "But I've had staff and the majority of them weren't willing!" You might feel quite correct about that, but again remember that this is also something that most executives overlook when it does, in fact, exist.

More ails society than the decline of economic conditions. It's been accompanied by decline in quality of education, in the moral quality of citizens as demonstrated by a rise in crime, a decline in available employment, etc. It can all be traced down to also a decline of willingness to observe what needs to be done about these and do those actions! But willingness is also one of the easiest traits to cultivate in the human resource.

Most of you reading this chapter will think that as an entrepreneur, or running a small company, you don't deal with government or society at large. And, while that is right, your company or group can be viewed as a little society that is part of a society, a state, and a nation. When you master how to deal with the willingness of your staff, your customers, your clients, providers, etc., you *will* make a difference!

So, let's take the viewpoint of a small business owner. What could he/she do?

First, one has to be able to spot the willing when procuring staff. How do we promote, find, hire, get onto production, and retain willing personnel? The keynote of these techniques can be summed up to applying two criteria:

1. Discover where the person operates emotionally on a daily basis and
2. Accurately establish the production record the employee has personally demonstrated by actual activities in the workforce.

Where the person operates emotionally can be explained simply by how much of a doer or a spectator the person is. Do they prefer to be a cause rather than an effect? Are they responsible for their actions or simply a victim of things that "happen" around them? The more causative and responsible the person is on the job, the higher the emotional level of the person. The higher their emotional level, the more willing they will prove to be in working with you.

The production record is simply an accurate account of how many or what volume they produce of something compared to the expected amount where they were working, no matter what they were doing. This also shows a record of willingness to get the job done.

Now, the question you need to ask yourself when you're advertising for new staff is: how do I attract people who operate at a high emotional level and have a high production potential?

Of course, as in any promotion, you want to utilize the channel where your ideal candidate is. For general staff, use websites, newspapers, etc., that reach the general public. If you're seeking staff with specialized skills, go to professional association websites, licensing board websites, etc.

What you say in your ads also helps attract people who might fulfill the criteria. For instance, an ad that says something like, "Progressive professional practice seeking upbeat front desk associate who loves dealing with people and has great attention to detail. Competitive performance based compensation plans available" will do more to attract folks who fulfill the criteria than a list of the functions that the person will be performing.

As with any promotion, the call to action is key to its success. In alignment with attracting people who fulfill the criteria, I'd make the call to action really "action" rather than a call to sit in front of the computer. Direct them to call a certain number to set up an appointment for an interview, instead of telling them to send you a resume.

When the person sets up an appointment to come for an interview, note if the person makes it on time, as you have your first piece of information: Do they do what they say they're going to do? If they don't but they call to say they can't make it, that tells you they don't have things under control, but they're trying. Not as much of a doer, but it might not totally rule them out. Of course, if they neither call nor show up, the person is likely to be a victim, so don't bother making another appointment if they somehow turn up in the future.

If the person shows up on time for the appointment, this fact merits that you invest a little bit of time with them. Greet them warmly and then have them fill out a job application form. The job application form should not be replaced by a resume. They are two very different sources of data and should never be confused. Use any generic job application form for your state. Usually, these are up-to-date with the labor laws.

Together with the job application form, hand out the job description of the position you are hiring for, so they know what they're applying for. The job description should have the position's purpose, result, skills needed, functions, production measurement, and quota of production expected within a stated probationary period. When the person signs the application form, they should understand what's expected of them.

This is also where any testing should be done (typing, IQ, personnel potential analysis, aptitude, etc.). Stay away from testing that isn't objective and doesn't give you data that aligns with the criteria. I've heard of testing that compares the person to a wolf or a lizard, and, honestly, I have no idea what you would accomplish with these!

In a larger company, a business owner or senior executive might not have spent any time on the hiring process. If you have an executive or employee in charge of hiring, they would've handled the above actions by themselves.

Once you have all the preliminary data gathered with the application, tests, and resume, an interview should take place to confirm or modify the data with personal, trusted observation. Once this is done, one would conduct a short review to conclude if you have a person either high or low in operational emotional level and if their past production record by inspection is high or low. With this, you should know by now if the person is willing or not.

If all the above has proven that you have potential willingness in this individual, the individual should be interviewed by the higher-ups to confirm the observations in the hiring process.

The more objective you are in your conclusions, the more certain you'll be that you're acquiring a willing individual for your staff. For example, deciding on the basis of "They were able to make happen 85% of the appointments in their previous job" rather than, "I did not care for her clothing or hairdo".

Let us suppose you've gotten this far and you're ready to offer them the job. Here's a little piece of advice, not always possible, but if you can: offer the job before you talk money. In as much as possible, talk money only as a necessary piece of paperwork that you have to do. Money is a factor, but it's not the reason a person should want a specific career. This is usually harder to do with university professionals who in many cases have big student loans and/or a costly image or lifestyle to keep up. Even in these cases, do not lose sight of the criteria you are looking for and don't let the negotiation drift from these.

Once you come to an agreement as to starting and when to start, and have shaken hands, done all paperwork, the next challenge begins: get them to justify their compensation as soon as possible.

While the two criteria we've been talking about are still valid and true in this part of the process, there's another one that will help you easily spot if you have a willing person. Do they correct the errors they make? Or do they continue to make them? You see, it takes willingness to correct oneself, too!

Ideally, you have a set of policies or guidelines in the form of a staff manual that applies to all your associates or employees, and another set of specialized guidelines for the job the person is taking. At this point, it's very important never to assume that because someone has gone to college or university that they know how to do a job. They didn't attend college or university to study how to work in your business or group, so don't assume they know in any detail how your company or group does things. If you don't have any manual like the one mentioned above, start making one, either on paper or video or both. As long as you communicate to the new employee what it is that you and/or your group needs and wants from that position clearly and completely, you'll be able to reap the benefits of the willingness you've seen this person has.

    The training period to make this position's performance viable varies. But this person's willingness will be preserved to the degree that their performance contributes to the group as much or more than the group contributes to them. There's an interesting law about contribution: it is an individual's contribution to others what makes them happy, not the other way around.

    Now, in order to be able to measure the production of this individual objectively, you should assign this person a statistic that he/she can keep track of and report every week. This is a production statistic, and it has to be consistent with what the person does. It measures the amount of work done or the performance on that particular job. For example, for a person who makes appointments with customers and is supposed to ensure they arrive, a good statistic would be "percentage of arrival".

    In closing, like any other resource, willingness should be sought, found, maintained, and nurtured. I hope with the above techniques you accomplish just that.

What's Next

Are you an entrepreneur or an enterprising individual? Have you ever felt making profits takes so much effort you don't get to enjoy life?

Does it seem that your associates or employees are not motivated or aligned with you? Do you think that if you want something done, you have to do it yourself?

Do you spend so much time busy with the business that you often miss important family functions?

Does your promotion have such poor results that you prefer not to do it?

My guide **"Eight Routes to Success"** will open the door to success for you. In it, you will discover:

- How to hire and organize associates or employees that understand what you're doing.
- How to invest money to attain higher production.
- How to improve your quality control even more.
- How to improve your image in the community.

**Go to www.EightRoutesToSuccess.com
and download the free guide now!**

Or you can request a free executive consultation at **www.ProfitsAndLife.com/FreeConsultation.**

I want to help you be more successful.

Good luck on your route to success!

Javier Guerrero
Master Business Consultant

Javier Guerrero was born and raised in Quito, Ecuador.

While his primary education took place in Ecuador, he finished his studies as a US Exchange student in the late 1970s, living in South Bend, Indiana. In addition to learning to speak English fluently, he developed a passion for international cultures and people from all walks of life.

He attended university in Brazil, graduating as a Forestry Engineer, which he practiced in the Amazon for some years.

In 1988 he was exposed to the Hubbard Management System and after realizing the potential it had to change business for the better, he decided to follow that as his career, knowing that helping others was the most worthwhile activity he would pursue. In 1989 he moved to the US to realize this purpose and he became a Certified Master Consultant from the Hubbard College of Administration International.

Since then he has trained and consulted hundreds of individuals and companies internationally using the above techniques to great success, and his students and clients continually attest to the great gain obtained under his care. Helping others understand and realize their potential as business people and individuals is his purpose in life.

Chapter 7

Five Principles to Step into Your Leader Within: Making a Difference for Yourself and Others
by Annette Fazio

As a presenter, my focus is on common sense and ground level information. Women like hearing me because I make sense and I'm funny; men like hearing me because I have a down to earth business logic and I'm funny. My programs are mostly directed to restaurateurs, small business owners, and woman in the business world. Regardless of your title, or responsibilities, it always boils down to perception.

How can you look at a situation differently in order to arrive at the best solution for yourself and others?

When you see things differently, you see things, well, er..., differently! Every situation is altered by the way you view it. If you're a business owner, your perspective may be from the bottom line. If you're a woman, you may see a more human viewpoint, and, if you are a restauranteur, you're probably working on the crisis of the day plan.

No matter which position you hold, most likely, you are in that position because you wanted to make a difference. You had a goal that was beyond financial. Sometimes, that ultimate goal gets lost in every day proceedings and the one thing that got you in motion to begin with gets lost. Achievement is something to be proud of. Accomplishment without joy, without balance, without feeling appreciated is a hard life. My goal is to bring an awareness to my audiences and a new way to view situations. What do you bring to the table to bring out the best in your coworkers, supervisor, your employees, the people you care about and still have fun in the process?

It's a concept, I'm sad to say, I didn't adopt until I was in my thirties. I didn't think it was possible for me to make a difference or that anyone would care if I tried.

Of course, it wasn't true. Everybody makes a difference, but, up until that point in time, that was the information my head was telling me.

I was a mother of two beautiful children, wrapped up in an alcoholic marriage, and stressed all of the time. I was living my life through the skewed moral compass of soap operas. I was discontent, to say the least, and knew I wanted more but had no clue what or where to start or worse, did I deserve to be happy at all or was I destined to a life of disaster. My history was a series of events, beyond my control, that looked like that was the path I was on.

I came close to death at two-and-a-half years old when hot boiling soup spilled on me and left me with horrendous scares, years of ridicule, medical care, and hospital time. I lost all the worldly possessions a seven-year-old can have, including my dog, when my home flared up into a fierce house fire. My father died suddenly when I was nine. My mother was diagnosed with lymphatic cancer when I was fifteen. The next five years, I was her primary caretaker and saw an up close and personal view of the ravages of cancer as I watched her spirit diminish with each experimental cancer drug therapy.

The carefree, spoiled teenage world I had my heart set on experiencing didn't happen. It would have been well worth it if she survived, but she lost the battle and died at the age of sixty-six; I was twenty.

I married the first man who asked. I was desperate to be saved from a life I was sure to be pure loneliness. After having two children, he promptly turned to alcohol and stopped supporting our family.

I had plenty of reasons, excuses, justification, validation, and support to be the perfect victim, and I might add, I was very good at it. If they gave awards for "perfect victim", I would have won, or at least been nominated.

One day, I had enough. I wanted life to be different for myself and my children. But where to start. I was never a stellar employee so I decided having my own business was the best solution; I'd be a nice boss and I wouldn't fire me.

Now that I had that detail settled, I had no idea what business I could start, especially with my financial limitations or what I was capable of accomplishing.

Looking back, I followed five principles that changed my world.

PRINCIPLE #1. You don't have to have all the answers to begin.

Start by assessing your skills.

What are you good at? Write it down.

I made a list of what I was good at. (Lists enable me to assess the situation with clarity.) What did I know? What did I like doing? It didn't matter how trivial it was. I could cook great Italian food so starting a home-based business was an option.

I made a marinara sauce. I got a few local store owners to carry it. I delivered my product faithfully every week. I learned that making one product was boring, so I added a few products to make it interesting. It didn't!

The home-based business was not in the least enjoyable, it

drained my energy.

That is an important sensation to notice. Does what you do, whether it's for fun or work, give you energy or does it drain you?

My products developed a following, and a few close friends encouraged me to open a restaurant. I personally didn't think that was a good idea. I had no interest in turning my life completely upside down and working 24/7. Not to mention my food business wasn't much fun and not very profitable either.

As my marriage deteriorated, the idea of owning my own restaurant became more appealing.

However, there were a few drawbacks. I had no training or business experience, never held a job as a manager, never worked in a restaurant, and then there was the small detail of having no money. What I had was the respect of the people who knew me. They trusted me and believed in me enough to encourage me to continue the quest and offered to co-sign a loan so I could get started.

Question: *What do you like to do, what gives you energy, what do you do that drains your energy. What are some of the things you do now that you love to do?*

PRINCIPLE #2. Take action, even if it's one small step at a time.

Do your research first.

Small steps will get you the furthest distance.

How do you perceive yourself as making a difference? On a community level, business level, or in your own family.

I had already concluded that business was the route I wanted to take, but you don't have to have a business to leave a permanent footprint.

Before I jumped at the offer to take someone else's money,

I did my research. The SBA (Small Business Administration) gave classes on the different aspects of business. I made a business plan and talked to bankers, restaurant owners and other business owners to get an idea of what I was jumping into. I met with an organization called SCORE, Senior Core of Retired Executives, an arm of the SBA created to help give direction to anyone who would like to go into business. He asked me questions, looked at my business plan, and absorbed my lack of credentials and experience. He looked me straight in the eye and, with as much conviction as he could drum up, said, "Do not go into this business. Find another way to move forward but do not do this." I walked out of there thinking, "What does he know!" He knew plenty. What he didn't know was my determination, my stubbornness, and the passion in my heart.

Another service of the SBA is the SBDC (Small Business Development Center) available in most cities. They offer classes on many topics, and it's free. Free is always good. It is an interesting place to start if you are not sure where your interests lie or which direction you would like to go in.

Question: *What projects have you pursued in the past only to abandon the idea? Did you move on to something else or just give up? Why?*

PRINCIPLE #3. Following your passion.

If you are heading in the right direction, the universe usually provides a way to support your plan. I was committed to the thought of the restaurant, but I wasn't going to slap it in just any location. At that moment in time, the perfect location became available because a restaurant closed at the same time I started looking for a location. It was walking distance to my daughter's middle school and the same for the high school my son attended.

The marriage ended, and I began my new life and opened Fazio's Italian Restaurant, September of 1986. Five years later, it tripled in size, and I opened two more pizza restaurants. I was so fascinated with the business end of the restaurant, taking care of my customers and making sure the restaurant was what I envisioned, that it became far more successful than I ever imagined. What the retired executive didn't know was me and what I was capable of; truthfully, either did I.

I was shocked to find out that I had become one of the ten million women who owned businesses in this country. Even more shocking, ess than four percent of that group took their business over the million-dollar mark, and I was one of them. Who knew!

The driving force to support my children is what got me into the restaurant business.

The passion that kept me excited was the business of bankers, business plans, and profit and loss statements to keep track.

Trust what you know! If you are following your passion, you don't tire. Yes, you will be exhausted at times, but your spirit doesn't tire. There were days that I thought "Oh my God, why did I do this?" Then I would spot something that kicked up a thought or an idea that I could use to improve the restaurant in some way and wham! I would get a burst of energy. Sometimes, it was a harsh reality to have the responsibility of employees, the business, be a single mom, and maintain my sanity. On the other hand, the question of my saneness has always been up for grabs. When customers heard my background, they would say I was very brave. My answer was it's either bravery or insanity. I'd put my money on insanity.

Question: *What signs or direction has the universe sent in your direction, currently or ever?*

PRINCIPLE #4. Treasure and respect your relationships.

It was a blessing to be able to hire a fabulous chef. He was a friend of a close friend, so I had trust in his character (more help from the universe). We became buddies instantly. I heard early on, "Take care of your friendship, and your business will survive." Friendships make the hard times bearable. The restaurant failure statistics are staggering. Ninety-five percent of new restaurants go out in the first year, five percent of those left standing go out within the next eighteen months, and five percent of those will close within the next five years. Early failure is usually due to lack of sufficient funding and poor management. The five-year mark comes from lack of everything else; not enough personal time to enjoy life and family, not enough money, too stressful, not as much fun as they thought it would be. The statistics for businesses outside of the restaurant world is about an eighty percent failure rate.

We got along, and we made each other laugh at the drop of a hat, which is a critical factor for me in any relationship. I realized almost immediately that he knew everything I didn't about the back of the house (the kitchen, ordering, scheduling, etc.). I was confident about the people end. After six months of working together, getting along and supporting each others' efforts, I invited him to be a partner.

He accepted. In the early years, we worked all the time. My kids were in the restaurant half their life, including homework time, and, eventually, they got paid to be there. I treated my employees fairly, as if they were friends. In turn, they treated our customers the same way.

Question: *How do you perceive yourself in the role as a family member, community member, in the business world? Do you see yourself as making a difference? Or an observer? Would you speak to and treat the people close to you the same* *way if you knew they wouldn't be there tomorrow?*

PRINCIPLE #5 Be grateful.

"Live every day as if it were your last!"

It's a common and probably overused cliché but it's a wise cautionary edict to follow. Today is the only day you have to work with. Make it count.

Plan for tomorrow, but keep in mind that today's decisions and actions will determine what your tomorrows look like.

We labor under the false illusion of having plenty of time. I lost my father to a fatal heart attack and my sister to a brain aneurism in a matter of minutes. The planes flying into the towers on 9/11 and collapsing killing thousands of people happened in less than two hours. The tower where the five firefighters I dedicated my book, *Finding the Leader Within*, to collapsed, and they perished in an instant before they could escape.

The point is you matter... at this very moment. You don't have to be better, or smarter, than you are right now. You have everything you need to make a difference. Look around you, and claim your own importance.

If you don't see the good in your life, make a gratitude list. Everyday come up with ten things to be grateful for. The more dejected I felt, the more things I needed to come up with. Some days, the number went up to one hundred before my spirits would lift. Trust me, by the time you get to one hundred, most everything you're unhappy about fades. If doesn't fade completely, it will be greatly diminished.

It's not a one-time deal either. I remarried a wonderful, loving man, but one month after we set a wedding date, he was diagnosed with a malignant tumor in his head. Yes, I know. Oy! Does it ever let up? There were ups and downs, and I started journaling October 1999, in the middle of one of the down spells. I followed Julia Cameron's book, *The Artist's Way*, to guide me, and I wrote three 8½" by 11" pages everyday. It became my daily meditation and my personal conversation with God. It helped me get my angry thoughts out of my head and enabled me to focus on what I still had to be grateful for, what I could do for myself, my husband, and, eventually, others. I was grateful for the opportunity to love him and give him the kindness and compassion I was too immature to give to my mother. I had a second chance to do it right. However, if I were asked, I would have skipped the opportunity, but wisdom comes when you didn't get what you wanted.

Together, we fought the disease two-and-a-half years, but he lost the battle in March 2001.

You must nurture yourself spiritually in addition to physically. If you don't, you're no good to anyone else. Through the discipline and process of journaling, it became abundantly clear that my history did not determine my destiny, and the way I view life changed forever.

Question: *Who and what are you grateful for? How can you honor what you have?*

Learn to live these five principles and let them take you to a life of joy and prosperity you can't begin to imagine.

Annette's Special Offer

Do you know you have a special "something" but you're not sure what it is?

My greatest belief is that if you focus on your strengths, your weaknesses become insignificant!

Allow me to share with you the same formula that took me from a struggling single mom to overcoming the prediction of "least likely to succeed" by starting a business and taking it over the million-dollar mark.

The best way to peek into your future is by grabbing my gift to you.

Go to www.FindtheLeaderWithin.com

and get

"A Simple Recipe to Powerful Results"

You will find a link inside this guide to schedule a FREE no-obligation discovery call.

I'm looking forward to supporting you in your special journey.

Annette Fazio

Annette Fazio dazzles audiences with her astonishing story of how she took four "noes" and turned them into "absolutely's". With no business experience, no industry knowledge, no culinary training, and no money, she transformed herself and her business into an award winning icon. Of the ten plus million women-owned businesses, she became one of the elite three-and-a-half percent that were able to take their business over the million-dollar mark. Her creativity complements her professionalism to produce effective and entertaining keynotes, seminars, and programs that are useful and inspiring to management and staff.

Her twenty-five years of leadership has made her uniquely qualified to teach, train, and motivate on all levels.

Her business experience includes a start-up specialty foods company, three restaurants, and a successful catering business. She developed and hosted a Boston cable cooking show, was an educator for Cordon Bleu, and, currently, speaks throughout the United States and internationally.

You can follow her at:

Website: http://www.AnnetteFazio.com/

Chapter 8

Change the World from the Front of the Room
by Tonya Hofmann

People always ask me two things:

1. **How and why did you get over the massive fears of speaking to become one of the top speakers in the world?** I just forced myself to stand up and talk. As often as I could and there was one major reason... I could change lives! I could cause tears in grown men, create waves of real change and give people insights that would transform their lives and businesses. Man... I was hooked!
2. **Who is your favorite speaker of all time?** People expect me to say someone famous, but it isn't. One of my members of the Public Speakers Association had never spoken before. She had fantastic information, and I was excited to hear her speak. She was on one of my virtual telesummits over the phone, and, for twenty-five minutes straight, she would say a sentence or two and start to hyperventilate! She would stop and start again... on and on for twenty-five minutes. When

she was done, she was so excited that she managed to do it even with massive fears. What was really neat is that usually listeners would get off the line since it was with a live listening audience but they didn't... I'm not sure if they were just wanting to wait for the train wreck or what but, afterward, they cheered and congratulated her! The next month, she did the telesummit again, and she only hyperventilated once and the last time. Never again. That is true success, and I love seeing people get out of their own way and just get it done!

Enjoy these tips, take them to heart, and **please**... create a "wow" moment for yourself every day. My goal is the same each year... to look back at myself the year before and to not recognize myself. This is when you know you have created real movement in your life, and you are no longer settling! HUGS and YIPPEE!

Tip 1

You have an expertise that can change lives, families, and businesses. How dare you keep it hidden and not share it! Your fate is to do just that... change lives, make money, and change more lives. You *are* fabulous, and the only thing holding you back is yourself and the mechanics of how to do it.

Tip 2

Let's do some numbers. Let's say you want to make $12,000 extra a year. With speaking, this becomes an easy success formula. If your average client spends a total of $1000 a year with you, you speak one time a month, find one new client a month, and, in twelve months, you have equaled $12,000!

Want more? Simply speak more times a month or increase your sales conversion to bring in more than one client at a time, and you can see how simple it is to make six figures speaking. Two clients per week, four speaking gigs a month equals $96,000 a year. Nice!

Tip 3

What kind of mindset do you have? The speaking world has changed ... it is now about being an entrepreneur.

The *employee mindset* says, "I'm worth so much. You must pay me for my time. I want to come, be done, and then go home!"

The *entrepreneur mindset* says, "I want to market myself, build relationships with everyone I meet so I can continue to help them forever, and continue the sales cycle. I know there are no guarantees but there are also no limits!"

To a speaker in today's market, it is essential to have the entrepreneurial approach.

Tip 4

The next mindset is to think like a billionaire.

There are three buckets of thought: regular, millionaire and billionaire.

I asked one of my billionaire friends, "Bill, why do you have a billion dollars and I don't? You just aren't that impressive, so I must be doing something wrong!"

Bill told me his secret: *Regular* people have one income stream so they only make a certain amount each year. *Millionaires* have multiple income streams, but *billionaires* have multiple income streams in every one of their income streams.

For example: Put on a webinar... It creates marketing opportunities, charge to attend, charge a sponsor, invite a guest speaker to market to their people, revenue share with the guest speaker, record the event, and make it into a CD/

DVD that you can resale over and over. Presto! Multiple income avenues from one activity.

Tip 5

Do you feel like you can never move forward? It is probably because you are trying to make things "perfect" before launching, sending, selling, etc. The real purpose of business is to help change people's lives and to make money changing those lives. So, any time you stop yourself, you also stop changing lives. Perfection will kill your speaking, presentations, sales conversion, opt-ins, traffic, etc. People want to do business with people they can relate to. Perfection is not only difficult to relate to but extremely boring.

Tip 6

I originally thought that, to become a speaker, I had to create the "perfect" presentation void of any mistakes. Then I uncovered some of the top million-dollar speakers in the world and listened to their unedited audios and videos. Guess what? They all said "um", mixed up their words, used wrong words, got sidetracked, stumbled and stuttered, and were *never* perfect. So, if they can make millions being imperfect, then why should I not follow suit?

Tip 7

What I see happen to many fabulous experts is they follow a formula that makes them sound and look like a robot or (even worse) like everyone else. Stop sounding like a robot spewing out words and putting on a presentation that is completely memorized word for word, slide by slide, hand motion to stage motion. The biggest mistake I see on stage is the speaker completely losing their own personality because they are trying so hard to recite a memorized speech, go over every point, read every slide word-for-word, and put on a "professional" image. This leads to no sales, no interaction, and zero connections to the audience.

Stop being afraid of being YOU!

Tip 8

Are you someone that people are drawn to know, or do you have to work hard at connecting? If people are naturally drawn to you, just ramp it up. Explode your smile and your reliability factor. If it takes some time for people to warm up to you, then go in knowing you have to work on each person you meet to build a fast working relationship. The faster you connect with people, the better your presentation and sales will be.

Tip 9

One aspect that is a game changer is how much you smile. Speakers often get caught up "teaching" and become so focused on getting their message across that they forget that you must get the audience to just plain like you. So, the speaker's smile vanishes until they are done teaching. Not only do you need to smile but your voice must smile, too, especially if you are on a virtual event where the audience can only hear your voice. Your voice must have changes in tone, which will keep your listeners engaged the whole time. This is imperative. Most of this engaging work is done in your facial expressions and your tone of voice. Reminder... no one likes to be lectured to. LOL

Tip 10

People want to do business with other people who are nice and encouraging. Personally, I only want people around me who are nice... no mean, grumpy, or just plain negative people are allowed. You want people to feel they can approach you, talk to you, ask you a question, and build a relationship with you. People want more positive energy in their lives, so be that driving force to change the world to a nicer place.

Tip 11

I have always found that doing nothing and waiting produces nothing, and, of course... nothing is ever accomplished. The more you do, the more things happen because action always equals more action. So go out and do something even if it is purely for marketing purposes. People need to see you doing, being in business, speaking, putting on events, creating products and services so that, when they are ready, they will think of you.

Tip 12

Whenever my stomach tingles with fear of doing something new, I make myself take action and force myself to do it. It is so exciting when you push through the fear to do your first presentation or first virtual event, and it is never as bad as you had played it out in your head. So go tackle a big, scary tingle today. Yes, today!

Tip 13

If you want to get booked to speak, you must be known. People must have heard of you and your message to want to bring you in to their group. It is imperative that you market yourself to become "famous". Fame simply means that, when someone is looking for an expert, they think of you. Now, we aren't talking "movie star" famous... but just the person someone else thinks of as being the perfect person to bring in for a subject.

Tip 14

To pick a brand, you first have to find out what your brand is right now. Yes... you already have a brand. It is what people think about you when they meet you. It is important to find out where you are starting from. If you have a chance, ask other speakers to give you some "real" feedback. You can find very helpful speakers at your local Public Speakers Association chapter meeting. Don't try to lead them where you want them to go, just let them give you the top three things off the top of their head that they thought, positive or negative, when they met you. It's hard to get people to critique you, but see if you can find someone. This will give you a base point to start from or to change.

Tip 15

It is incredibly important especially in the beginning to say "Yes" to all the opportunities that come your way even if you don't feel ready. There are a lot of teleconferences (events over the phone), webinars (events on the computer with video and/or Power Points), and other new formats coming online now that you can be part of, and, since they are all virtual, that means no travel costs. These are perfect to get your message out, do lots of practicing, and are truly amazing lead generators (where people who follow you on social media, opt in to your email newsletter, and contact you for more information or a strategy session).

Tip 16

I want to leave you with this.
YOU have a message.
YOU can help thousands.
YOU can change the world.
YOU have a responsibility to change YOUR life and the lives of others!

So what are you waiting for? Don't wait any longer. Take the leap, change tomorrow, make an impact, make some money, be able to give money away, stand and be proud, stand and be loud, stand and be HEARD!
Today is YOUR Day... Don't let another day sneak past you.
I believe YOU can do it, so now it is YOUR turn to believe YOU can do it!

Tonya's Special Offer

"Change the World from the Front of the Room! How to Get Booked and Paid to Speak!"

http://tonyahofmann.com/free/

Listen to this full training on:

-How you can be a speaker
-How to get booked to speak on stage
-How to make money as a speaker
-Changes in the speaking world you need to know about

Tonya will walk you through her vast knowledge of the speaking world so that you too can go out and change lives for others and yourself!

Tonya Hoffman

- CEO & founder of the Public Speakers Association
- Globally Sought After Speaker
- Host of Tonya Hofmann's Fabulous TV Show
- Best Selling Author of 6 Books
- Winner: International eWomenNetwork '08 Business Matchmaker of the Year
- Winner: 2015 Females are Fabulous Award
- Finalist 2015 Central Texas Women of Influence
- Winner: 2015 The Sip & Chat Movement Empowerment Award for Best Speaker

Chapter 9

Don't just Survive, Thrive!
by Mari Muscio

The wait was unbearable. The mammogram detected a suspicious tumor. I hadn't had a mammogram in over five years, which some might consider ironic considering I own a boutique specializing in mastectomy products. I was reluctant to have a mammogram so I initially opted for breast thermography. Breast thermography is digital infrared imagery which uses ultrasensitive medical infrared cameras and sophisticated computers to examine and create high resolution images of the breast. It can be used to detect early signs of breast cancer.

My report found something suspicious in my breast, and the doctor recommended I make an appointment to receive a mammogram. My mammogram soon revealed that what the (DII) saw was a cyst. My doctor urged that I have an ultrasound and biopsy to rule out cancer. I must admit I was not used to having medical tests done, and certainly did not want to be diagnosed with breast cancer. In addition to the mammogram, I received an MRI to make sure that there were no other abnormalities other than what was found. The results of the MRI found a cyst in my liver. I went from being nervous to being in a state of fear while waiting for the test results.

At this point, I could empathize with my clients who were newly diagnosed. The Buddhist saying "become the master of your mind, do not let your mind master you" continued to reverberate in my mind. Despite attempting to remain calm, I spent the week in fear waiting for my results. I received a call from my doctor at 5:00 pm on a Friday, and he informed me that I did not have cancer, but that I should get checked in six months to make sure nothing changed. I did receive yet another ultrasound and the report was good. This experience has led me to become proactive, taking preventative steps by living a healthy lifestyle and getting yearly mammograms and/or ultra sound of breasts and self-exam. I enjoy attending fundraising events in support of cancer research. Such causes provide education and awareness.

In the face of this breast cancer epidemic, one of the biggest challenges women face today is the increased probability of being diagnosed. My hope is that with education about breast cancer, women can become empowered, and, if diagnosed, my message is **"Don't just survive, thrive!"** As a certified mastectomy fitter for over thirteen years, I have seen many patients in a state of shock and, in some cases, barely able to function. A recently diagnosed mother stated, "I fell apart; I literally could not get out of bed."

I believe that the more knowledge women have of this epidemic, the more empowered they will become. As women, we must not just survive, we must thrive. Knowing the facts about breast cancer, including who is at risk, will better position women to understand what preventative steps to take. According to the American Cancer Society's website, about one in eight women will develop breast cancer during their lifetime. Almost 247,000 new cases of breast cancer are estimated to occur during 2016 within the United States. At some point in one's life, one is likely to know a woman diagnosed with breast cancer. She may be a family member, friend, or co-worker and could be of any age. The National Cancer Institute website states that most women with breast cancer do not have family history of the disease. Only thirteen percent of women diagnosed have a relative, usually a mother, sister, or daughter, with breast cancer.

For almost a decade and a half, I have worked with women who have survived breast cancer, when I enquire of one of my patients whether breast cancer runs in their family, more often than not their answer is "no." Thus, since breast cancer is usually not hereditary, self-exams can be critical in reducing your risk of cancer. The American Cancer Society recognizes breast self-exams as an optional screening tool. They should be done once a month at home, as well as with your doctor at an annual exam.

Unfortunately, no woman is exempt from the possibility of having breast cancer. My own personal belief is that eating a clean diet consisting of organic fruits, vegetables, meats, and grains, as well as taking steps to use nontoxic products in the home may help reduce your risk of cancer, but also aid in remaining healthy overall. Moreover, arming yourself with an understanding of this disease is vital for early prevention, and knowing what to do if you or someone you know is diagnosed. If a woman is diagnosed with breast cancer and requires a mastectomy, there are products that must be obtained before, during, and after surgery. The insurance companies, hospitals, cancer centers, breast care coordinators, and oncologists provide a list of places to go for mastectomy products. For example, the list will include durable medical equipment stores where wheelchairs, oxygen tanks, and hospital beds are among the many items available for purchase. Most of the women I work with do not prefer that type of environment. Rather, given that women have a choice of where to go, they prefer a more private and specialized environment, with a warm, caring, experienced staff. Some department stores offer mastectomy fittings, but newly diagnosed women feeling vulnerable may not want to be served with the general public at a department store. The department stores often require women to pay up front for product and will bill their insurance. The insurance company will reimburse the patient at a later date.

If a woman has had a double mastectomy from breast cancer which is the removal of both breasts, she will require two prosthetic silicone breasts and two bras which have a pocket for the prosthesis. The cost is around $828 dollars. Given all the medical expenses she will have to pay from surgery, the cost of paying up front for prosthesis and bras can create a financial burden. Lastly, a boutique specializing in mastectomy products is a good choice for women who have had breast cancer. Most boutiques bill insurance, and the only money out of pocket is a deductible, co-pay, or an upgrade, which is the amount not covered by insurance. The upgrade is nominal. Boutiques for women with breast cancer are comfortable, safe, and caring. Make sure they are able to bill your insurance company, that they are certified with The American Board of Orthotics which sets high standards, and that the store has certified mastectomy fitters.

A woman who will undergo a mastectomy will need a post-surgical garment prior to surgery. She should call to confirm if the product is covered under her insurance plan. Not all garments are covered. She will wear the garment for at least one week. The garments have a pouch for the drainage tube which stay in for a week. I recommend purchasing two garments since it can be difficult having to wash one often during the week.

Two weeks after surgery is the ideal time to begin wearing a post-surgical bra which is soft against the skin. There is usually some swelling of the chest wall at this time. The post-surgical bra has pockets for soft pillow like breasts and is a comfortable option before a regular bra can be worn. Six weeks after surgery, a woman can be fitted for regular bras and prosthesis. Most insurance companies cover prosthetics every other year and two bras a year. A prescription or authorization is required for coverage. It is best to call your insurance company and confirm coverage.

Women must confirm coverage for a wig which she will need if going through chemotherapy. It is best to choose a wig or cranial prosthesis prior to chemotherapy. Once chemotherapy begins, she may not feel well enough to shop for a wig. It is a good idea to purchase a wig from a boutique specializing in products for women who are going through chemotherapy. Most shops will bill insurance for a wig and will confirm coverage. Buying a wig on the internet may not be a good idea. I have many clients who purchased a wig without being able to try it on, and they were disappointed. Wigs can't be returned.

I am co-owner of a boutique in San Diego county which provides mastectomy products to women. I acquired The Brighter Side from a breast cancer survivor in 2003. I wanted to own a business that could help make women's lives better.

I have been a caring and compassionate person all of my life. In junior high school, I attended a service-oriented church. We would go down to orphanages in Mexico with supplies and toys for the children. We also visited the elderly in assisted living facilities. In high school, I was a volunteer candy striper at Scripps Hospital. In 2003, I created The VAS Memorial Fund which provides funds for uninsured women. Lastly, I am a co-owner of two professional women's tennis tournaments, The Carlsbad Classic in Carlsbad, California, and The San Antonio Classic in Texas. The Carlsbad Classic hosted two charity events in 2015, raising thousands of dollars for both Operation Underground Railroad, which stops sex trafficking of children, and The Freedom Foundation, which provides prosthetics for wounded vets.

Early detection and prevention is critical to surviving breast cancer if diagnosed. My most important message is that women familiarize themselves with available resources, navigate through the medical system, and know what their insurance benefits are.

Let's not just survive; let's thrive.

Mari Muscio

Mari Muscio is an entrepreneur and co-owner of The Brighter Side, a boutique for women with cancer providing mastectomy products, wigs, head coverings, and skin care. Although The Brighter Side is a for profit business, she is founder of the VAS, a nonprofit for uninsured women with cancer providing products and services at little or no cost.

Mari co-owns two professional women's tennis tournaments. The Carlsbad Classic and The San Antonio Classic. The Carlsbad Classic, an inaugural Women's Tennis Association (WTA) event, has designated Warrior Foundation-Freedom Station as an official charity partner.

She serves on the board of directors for Anova Education a school for students with Autism and Asberger Syndrome.

Mari's interests include running long distance, circuit training, skiing, horseback riding, and traveling. She has traveled extensively and studied in Guadalajara, Mexico, and Japan. Mari holds a BA in International Relations from The University of San Diego. Her motto is "Don't Just Survive, Thrive!"

To interview her about her boutique, go to:

www.MyBrighterSide.com.

To find out about her products and services, you can contact the store for a free consultation at 619-461-7565 in La Mesa, California, or 858-481-7565 in the popular design district on Cedros Avenue in Solana Beach, California.

Chapter 10

Create a Healthy Home, Energize Your Life, and Change the World
by Bonnie Bradford

My own personal awareness and profound interest about the connections between health and the environment started when I was a young child. I remember hearing my mom talk about how her mother had died at age forty-four when my mom was just sixteen years old.

My grandmother, Pauline, worked in a factory that made "glow in the dark" radium clocks and wristwatches. Her job was to paint the radium onto the dials. To keep the brush wet, the women typically licked the brushes to keep them pointed. She, like many others, developed radium poisoning and died at an early age of kidney failure from occupational exposure.

This is a tragedy that illustrates the very personal connection between our health and our environment—in this case exposure to chemical toxins. It is also a political connection. As with the tobacco industry, the radium dial industry knew that ingestion was detrimental to human health long before any actions were taken to protect workers. Eventually, the truth came out, and some changes were made—if only to warn people of the dangers. For many people, like my grandmother, it was too late.

While occupational exposure to radium may sound like something from the distant past, there are many harmful chemicals and toxins we are exposed to on a regular basis, including ones found in most homes in the United States. One of the first steps we can take is to become aware of what these substances are, and where they are commonly found, so that we can reduce our risks.

Through HealthHomeToday.com, one of my main goals is to help connect people with the information and knowledge they need and raise awareness about the many advocates and activists who are working on our behalf. I also want to help people spread the word and educate their families, friends, and communities, and ultimately help change the world and save the planet on which we all depend.

Environmental Health is a Key to Wellness

Back when I was in my 20s, I knew that I wanted to work in public health, wellness, healing, and/or medicine. I was also drawn to working with low-income people in need of basic healthcare and social services and found great satisfaction in doing this. My first trip to a developing country back in 1983 was to Haiti. As soon as I got off the plane in Port-au-Prince (the capital city), the sights, smells, vibrant colors, markets, art, music, and the city itself were overwhelming.

I knew within a few days of experiencing life in Haiti that I wanted to specialize in environmental health, beginning with basic water, sanitation, garbage, and air quality. I realized that the environment, which also includes potentially harmful chemicals, has a profound impact on human health, especially to the most vulnerable including women, children, and the elderly. This is a powerful set of lenses through which I have come to see the world.

After spending time in Haiti, Egypt, Kenya, India, and elsewhere, I went on to study International Public Health at Johns Hopkins University with a focus on Environmental Health. I have spent the past thirty plus years of my life being involved in community and environmental health, which remains one of my passions.

I recently retired after more than ten years on staff at the World Bank Institute. I am excited about starting HealthyHomeToday.com so that I can help people, especially those facing health challenges, live their healthiest lives. My mission critical message is also to help raise awareness about, and help people take steps to reduce or eliminate, our daily exposures to harmful chemicals and substances that are often found in our food, water, air, and environment.

Home as Sanctuary

Most of us strive to create a home that is comfortable and a safe haven—and even a sanctuary—for ourselves, our families, and our friends. Ideally, our home is a place where we can enjoy life in a healthy atmosphere that is warm and inviting. Sometimes the reality is quite different, but most people aim to enjoy peace, calm, and positive energy in our home environment and our home life.

Our home can also be seen as a reflection of who we are at a given point in time in all dimensions—body, mind, and spirit. Many people see the home as a representation of the self. And for many of us, our homes—just like ourselves—are a constant work in progress.

While we may not have as much control as we would like over what goes on in our work places, our communities, and in the wider world, we usually do have more control over what goes on in our home environment, including what we bring into our homes through our household purchases.

And we don't need to spend a fortune to create a healthy home. Many changes we can make today will actually save us money in the short and long term. And, if necessary, we can make changes gradually. We can also save on our health costs by living a life with fewer toxins and a higher quality of life.

We can make our dollars count by not buying products that are potentially harmful to our health and the health of the planet. Companies and corporations typically follow the money. We can send a powerful message by buying or making our own safer, non-toxic products. With each passing year, advocacy and activist groups are becoming stronger and more effective as more people get involved. Calls to action for environmental justice and for each of us to help create a healthier, safer, and sustainable planet have become a global movement.

Let's look at some of the specifics now.

What are Home Toxins and Where are They Found?

Many people assume that chemicals used to make consumer products sold in the United States are tested for safety and regulated—but, actually, most are not. Over 80,000 chemicals are currently on the market, and the United States Environmental Protection Agency (EPA) has required very few of these to be tested for their possible impacts on human health. Many of these chemicals have made their way into our homes and our environment.

Here are just three of the many common toxic chemicals and substances found in many homes. Their potential health effects—alone and in combination with one another—can have negative and, in some cases, devastating and long-lasting impacts on our endocrine, cardiovascular, respiratory, reproductive, neurological, immune, and/or other systems of the body.

1. Bisphenol A (BPA): This is an industrial chemical found in some plastic bottles, some plastic food and drink containers, and many canned food and beverage linings. BPA has more recently been found to be present in the coating of most cash register receipts.

Health Linkages: BPA is a synthetic estrogen that can disrupt the endocrine system. BPA has been linked to breast and reproductive system cancers, infertility, diabetes, obesity, early-onset puberty, and ADHD.

How Many People Affected: United States Centers for Disease Control and Prevention (CDC) surveys testing for BPA have found BPA in the bodies of almost every person tested. While some companies have replaced BPA with BPS and other plastics, recent studies show that BPS and other plastics can be just as damaging to human health as BPA.

2. Parabens: These chemicals are commonly found in cosmetics and personal care products. They are also found in some processed foods (in the form of propyl paraben).

How Many People Affected: The United States Centers for Disease Control and Prevention (CDC) found parabens in more than ninety percent of people they studied and tested. Unlike in the United States, parabens are not allowed in food sold in the European Union.

Health Linkages: Parabens have been linked to possible health risks, including their potential to disrupt hormones and the endocrine system, and they can lead to adverse effects on the body's reproductive and immune systems.

3. Perfluorinated chemicals (PFCs), including perflurooctanoic acid (PFOA) and polytetrafluoroethylene (PTFE – also known as Teflon): These chemicals have been widely used to repel water, grease, and stains in food, carpets, clothing, and furniture. PFCs are commonly found in nonstick cookware, some food package linings (such as many microwave popcorn bags and pizza boxes), carpet and upholstery treatments, and water-and-stain repellent coatings. Chemicals being used by some companies to replace various types of PFCs (including PFOA substitutes) may not be any safer for people or the planet.

Health Linkages: PFCs have been linked with kidney and testicular cancer, elevated cholesterol levels, obesity, and negative effects on the thyroid, liver, reproductive, and immune systems.

How Many People Affected: PFCs have been found in nearly all individuals tested in United States federal public health studies. PFCs are widely found in people's bodies, in the home, and in the environment. PFCs are highly persistent chemicals that tend to accumulate and remain in our bodies for years.

What Can You Do to Get Rid of Home Toxins Fast?

Fortunately, you can reduce your risks of health problems from these and many other toxins by easy steps you can take around the home. Here are five action steps, with a few ideas in each one, to help you make major progress in reducing your exposure.

Action Step 1. Clear the Cleaning Products

In the United States, many of our cleaning products contain hazardous ingredients. Most of these products are not necessary and, in fact, can be dangerous to human health.

With cleaning products, we need to get back to basics. It's important to learn how to recognize hazardous ingredients and get them out of our homes. Safe and effective cleaning products can be made using simple recipes using ingredients like white vinegar, baking soda, and fresh lemons.

If you don't have time to make your own products, you can purchase them instead. The Environmental Working Group (EWG), a non-profit research and advocacy group, is an excellent resource. EWG's online database rates thousands of cleaning products to help us make safer choices for ourselves and our families.

In addition to cleaning products, use a vacuum cleaner with a HEPA (high efficiency particulate air) filter. Household dust often contains a mix of hazardous toxins, including pesticides, parabens, and flame retardants that are found in household products and what we bring into the home on our shoes and clothing.

By using a HEPA vacuum—and taking additional precautions in the case of cleaning up lead dust found in older homes and brought in from the outside—we can make a tremendous difference in reducing toxic exposures. This is especially true for small children who spend much of their time on the floor, where a lot of household dust settles.

Action Step 2. Tackle Your Kitchen Toxins

Avoid nonstick pots and pans. This way, you avoid toxic chemicals (like PFCs and PFOAs mentioned earlier) that are released when the pots and pans heat up on the stove or in the oven.

If you currently have nonstick pots and pans and cannot afford to get new ones right away, plan to replace them with safer choices as soon as you start to see scratches or chips in the finishing coat. Try not to use high heat while cooking until you can replace the pots and pans. Do not give these away to other people to use and do not donate them.

Stainless steel (not aluminum), cast iron, and some enamel-coated cookware are generally better choices for cookware than non-stick pots and pans.

The safety of new ceramic coatings, developed after the dangers of Teflon were widely publicized, depends on how they are manufactured. Many new types of coatings are made with a variety of chemicals that have not yet been adequately tested. In general, it's best to use caution with all types of non-stick coatings.

Also avoid plastic containers for storing food and for heating up food in the microwave. BPA and other plastic-related toxins can leach out from these containers into food and bottled water.

Action Step 3. Is it Really Personal Care?

Personal care products include hair care products like shampoos and conditioners, deodorants, body lotions, and soaps. Avoid parabens, phthalates, and artificial fragrances.

An individual artificial fragrance can contain hundreds of chemicals, some of which can cause health issues, especially for people with asthma or respiratory problems.

Personal care products, and especially cosmetics, constitute a huge industry with intense marketing efforts in all forms of media, including broadcast, online, and print. Products deemed "natural" or "green" in marketing are often anything but healthy.

You can make your own personal care products at home, or check the Environmental Working Group (EWG) online database for safety ratings of personal care products, including cosmetics.

Action Step 4. How to Really Quench Your Thirst

Water is essential for our health and well being. It's important to stay hydrated, and drinking good quality water throughout the day can help us flush toxins out of our bodies.

Most of us are fortunate to have access to tap water for drinking in our homes. In general, tap water is tested and regulated for certain contaminants, while most bottled is not. In addition, most bottled water is in plastic containers, which should be avoided when possible.

It's important to know what's coming out of your tap. Drinking water utilities are required to provide consumers with reports (generally available online) of what is in the water. Water testing kits can also provide useful information.

These are starting points to know whether or not additional steps, such as filtering, are needed and what kind of filtration or treatment is needed. In many cases, a simple and inexpensive carbon filter on the kitchen tap can significantly reduce many potentially harmful contaminants in the water.

A simple and relatively inexpensive shower or bathwater filter to remove chlorine should ideally be installed in each shower or bathtub used for showering or bathing. Chlorine is easily absorbed through the skin and if the shower is hot and steamy, chlorine can be inhaled directly into the lungs, with the potential to cause respiratory and breathing problems, and make asthma symptoms worse.

Action Step 5. Take a Deep Breath and Say...

The United States Environmental Protection Agency (EPA) has found that indoor air levels of many pollutants can be at least two to five times, and sometimes up to a hundred times, higher than outdoor levels. And it is estimated that many people spend as much as ninety percent of their time indoors.

Contaminants come from a variety of sources inside the house and can be brought in from the outside on shoes and clothing. Because we generally keep doors and windows closed, and many homes are so well sealed with modern windows and doors, these contaminants can build up in the air.

Potential sources of indoor air pollution include many standard house cleaning and personal care products, as well as many commercial air fresheners, dryer sheets, flame retardants, plastic used to encase dry cleaned clothing, as well as animal dander, pollen, and pesticides.

There is a lot we can do to help clean the indoor air. Simply opening a window to ventilate the house for a period of time every day will help.

NASA has found that many houseplants can help filter the air in our homes as well as increase oxygen and help humidify the air. It's important to select ones that are safe if you have small children or pets.

A wide variety of air filters and purifiers are also available. Tests of air quality can help determine whether or not these are necessary and which ones to consider purchasing.

What's Next?

These Five Action Steps can help you on the road to get rid of many home toxins.

So what's next?

Make the decision to create a healthier home environment for you and your family. The steps outlined here can help you feel better, gain energy, and empower you to help change the world for the better.

I also want to help you take the easiest, fastest, and most effective steps you need, based on your main health concerns and issues, your lifestyle, and your timeframe.

I'm on a mission to help you, and your family, have a healthy home today. And I also want to help you change the world and save the planet.

Contact me to schedule a free 20-minute strategy session to help determine your next best actions to begin seeing health and life changing results today.

Send an email to: Bonnie@HealthyHomeToday.com to schedule your session. I look forward to hearing from you.

Don't put it off another day.

Cheers to Your Health,

Bonnie

Bonnie Bradford

Bonnie Bradford is an International Environmental Health Professional with more than thirty years of experience in community and environmental health and international development.

Bonnie has a Master of Public Health (MPH) degree from Johns Hopkins School of Public Health. She majored in International Public Health with a focus on Environmental Health. She completed a Bachelor of Arts (BA) degree at The George Washington University in Education and Human Development with a major in Human Services.

She has a passion for community, environmental, and international health and education. She lived and worked in Honduras for five years. She has been a staff member and consultant to international organizations, local governments, non-profits, and charities. Her technical specialties include water, sanitation, housing and health linkages, health education, communications, and lead poisoning prevention.

Before entering the field of international public health, she was a community health educator in several Washington, DC, community-based public health clinics serving low-income and minority clients.

Bonnie has written and edited numerous books, monographs, articles, and newsletters on public health and development topics, and was co-editor of *Down to Earth: Community Perspectives on Health, Environment, and Development*, a book of case studies, including several on environmental justice, published by Kumarian Press.

Chapter 11

Solving a Worldwide Epidemic
by Kim Dandurand

In 1997 I began questioning the effects of electromagnetic radiation being emitted from cell phones and how it may be impacting the health of my family. With the introduction of computers and cell phones in my home, I became suspicious of the increased health related problems my children were experiencing. Not knowing what the cause was, I started what has become a twenty-year investigation into the effects of electromagnetic radiation on the human body.

During the years that followed, I have been relentless in my research; not only into the dangers of cell phone radiation, but into possible ways to protect the body from the damage that accrues with the use of wireless technologies. Acknowledging the impact and convenience of these products, not only in the business community, but to individuals as well, I knew I couldn't stop the production of these product. However, I did resolve to find a way to reduce the impact of this harmful radiation. The journey has not been easy.

The first reaction I received was that of defiance. People thought I was suggesting they give up the convenience of their phones and computers. Not only did I understand their reluctance, I agreed with it. Giving up on the technology was not an option. I also knew that, in order for anyone to support me and my ideas, I would have to come to this endeavor with the attitude that I didn't have to break the technology for a solution to work. With this strategy in place, I partnered with scientists around the world.

In order to understand the problems with cell phone radiation, you must first have a basic knowledge of how the technology works. Mobile phones work like a two-way radio, transmitting through a network of fixed antennas sending and receiving information. Radiofrequency waves are nearly the same as electromagnetic fields. The body is no stranger to electromagnetic fields because the earth itself has one that is constantly interacting with our body. According to Dr. David Hamilton, even the heart responds to these fields. When you have electromagnetic fields, which occur naturally, which are coherent, the radiation looks like a smooth black wave pattern. But, when the electromagnetic frequencies are manmade, they are fuzzy and incoherent, breaking though the body's DNA. Another way to visualize this is to imagine barbed wire ripping though your body; that would be similar to the incoherent manmade electromagnetic frequency.

As I continued my quest for answers, I turned to nature. Believing that the answer was to find a way to convert the manmade electromagnetic wave into a coherent wave, I worked with experts and scientists to find a solution. I explored the use of ground minerals and trace element derived from a highly paramagnetic rock I'd discovered; I recognized its amazing properties and felt the compounds might provide some answers. I hypothesized that using the crystalline structure may work in neutralizing the negative effects of the man made frequency.

With this in mind, I funded a research and development

program at Quantum Biology laboratories in Northport, New York. Experiments proved that human DNA reacted adversely to incoherent manmade electromagnetic fields emanating from a cell phone while recovering from heat shock. Measurements were taken of the time it took for the DNA to recover from heat shock exposure to the EMF emitted by cell phones. Tests on human DNA proved that the formulation I created, when placed on a cell phone, neutralized the effect of the EMFs on the human DNA when exposed and allowed a hundred percent recovery from heat shock. This discovery was extraordinarily significant. The natural coherent fields from the rock crystals had successfully harmonized the incoherent EMFs from the cell phone and retuned them to be coherent, natural frequencies; no longer causing adverse reaction to living tissue.

There is an estimated 6.9 billion cell phone subscribers globally and the number is growing. Although there has been much controversy over the safety of cell phones and wireless technology, the scientific community has not come up with a clear consensus. With concerns over cell phone danger mounting, the World Health Organization (WHO) was tasked with the responsibility of compiling all of the research data and reporting on its conclusions. In 2012, the WHO reported that they were changing the classification of cell phone emissions to "possibly carcinogenetic", which put it into the same category as lead and engine exhaust. They felt the damage built up over time and suggested that the public keep the phone away from the head. The group that reported on the dangers, which included thirty-one scientists from fourteen countries, found there was enough evidence to change the classification. Additionally, it stated that one of the biggest problems is that environmental factors take decades of exposure to truly see the consequences. Essentially, the public had been experimenting on themselves from the day cell phones and similar products were introduced.

Dr. Keith Black, chairman of neurology at Cedars-Sinai Medical Center in Los Angeles, stated, "Microwave radiation from cell phones essentially cook the brain", in addition to the possible development of cancer and brain tumors. Dr. Black also said, "There could be a whole host of effects including memory function." The concerns for children are even greater. Children's skulls are thinner and therefore cell phone radiation has a greater impact.

Dr. Henry Lai, research professor in bioengineering at the University of Washington, also has concerns. After studying radiation for more than thirty years, Lai suggests that consumers should receive adequate warnings about the long-term exposure to cell phone radiation and how it could possibly cause cancer.

Manufactures of cell phones include a heath safety warning to keep your phone at least fifteen to twenty-five millimeters (depending on the type of phone) from your head at all times. This warning however, is in very fine print that most studies show is not read by the consumer.

Dr. Debra Davis, author of *Disconnect*, has warnings as well. In addition to her agreement that cell phones are extremely dangerous, she has specific concerns about pregnant mothers and baby's in the womb. She warns that the use of cell phones and laptop computers has a high possibility to harm both mother and baby. Another target population of Dr. Davis is the damage that is done to sperm with men who are trying to conceive families. Not only is the sperm count affected but the health of the sperm as well. She makes a correlation between the tobacco and asbestos industries to the current cell phone companies. She works extensively with other countries, including India, Finland, UK, France, Israel, Russia, Spain, Italy, Taiwan, Germany, and the US, and suggests that precautionary warnings about cell phone radiation be announced through the governing bodies.

The American Academy of Pediatrics (AAP) has recently published an opinion paper warning parents not to have their small children play with cell phones.

In May of 2015, the international EMF Scientist Appeal, comprised of two hundred peer-reviewed scientists, responded to these growing concerns of cancer, reproductive health, fetal development, children's health, and electromagnetic sensitivities by asking the UN, WHO, and UNEP to address the concerns of the public health crisis related to cell phones, wireless devices, and wireless utility meters.

These are just an example of the reports that have kept me passionate about my progress in creating a solution to the negative effects of cell phone radiation. I have created several products that neutralize the harmful effects of cell phone radiation. My flagship product is the Aulterra Neutralizer. Unlike other products on the market, the neutralizer has been shown to neutralize the effects of manmade electromagnetic damage of human DNA. While some products claim to block the radiation, a device like a cell phone would severely affect its performance. In terms of products claiming to absorb, any device that genuinely absorbed EMF's would become saturated and no longer function. When I created the Neutralizer, the most significant criteria I recognized was that the product could never be practical if it relied on either blocking or absorbing radiation. Instead, it had to neutralize the EMF's. I've spent much of my life on this mission of protecting the world from the dangers of EMFs and have truly created the only product that has been tested and proven, to dramatically reduce and eliminate the harmful effects EMFs produce. My life goal is to have my Neutralizers on at least two billion cell phones, and, with the help of partners around the world, I am well on my way to accomplishing that goal.

Kim's Special Offer

We hope that you learned something from our chapter, as our **free gift**, we would like to send you one free Aulterra Neutralizer.

Here is how you redeem it:

1. Go to our website: www.Aulterra.com
2. Click on the store link
3. Add one Neutralizer Single to your cart
4. Enter Promo Code: MCMAultSingle
5. Check out and receive your free Neutralizer Single in the mail!

Limit one per customer

(You will need to enter credit card or PayPal information, but you will not be charged.)

Kim Dandurand

Inventor and developer of the Aulterra Neutralizer, Kim Dandurand has become one of the leading authorities in the field of electromagnetic damage on human DNA.

Through true dedication, Kim has obtained over 20 years of experience and research in the field of EMF Radiation. Kim Dandurand has worked with respected and world-renowned scientists to protect consumers from the ever-increasing dangers of technology. He became passionate about this pursuit when he observed changes in the health and behavior of his children as various EMF producing technologies entered his home. He has spoken and educated internationally in over fifteen different countries and has been featured in countless articles and appearances on TV and radio throughout his career. His revolutionary products are currently in use in over sixty countries.

As president and CEO of Aulterra International, an Idaho-based bio-technology company, Mr. Dandurand holds a U.S. patent with forty-three claims on his products. Additionally, the results of the Neutralizer have been published in several scientific, peer-reviewed journals. The Neutralizer creates a scientifically significant reduction in harmful radiation when used on cell phones and other electronic devices.

Chapter 12

How to Keep Your Pets Happy and Healthy
by Mary Stevenson

Pets enhance our lives on so many levels. When we have them in our lives and as part of the family, we want to do everything we can to make them as happy and healthy as possible.

Most of the time, we think of keeping our dogs healthy by feeding them a high quality, pure food diet and making sure they get plenty of exercise.

Every breed has their own special needs, and it is very important to have the right diet and exercise program for your dog.

However, there are other aspects of your dog to examine. Looking at your dog in this different way can help to shift and change things that you may not have thought of before.

Step 1: Connect with Your Dog

How do I connect with my dog?

Walking your dog is quality time for the two of you to spend together. Both of you will get exercise and share an activity. The same is true for dog training classes. This is a time when your focus is on your dog, and he appreciates that very much. It gives you and your dog an opportunity to work your minds as well as your bodies and strengthen your bond.

Another way of connecting is by relaxing with, cuddling, and petting your dog. This is very beneficial for both the dog and the owner. Studies have shown that when people are petting animals, this stimulates the production of our 'good hormones' throughout our bodies and brings on a very peaceful, happy feeling. Of course, you and your dog will feel the love you have for each other when spending this quiet time together.

We can connect with our dogs on a mind level when our minds are quiet and open. You do this by relaxing and becoming aware of what your mind is thinking about. Then allow all of those thoughts to fade away. Focus on our breathing and when thoughts pop into your mind, just acknowledge them and let them go. You can continue to do this until your mind is quiet.

Once your mind is quiet, you are then open to receive messages from your animals. Maybe you have let your dog outside, sat down to watch television, then all of a sudden you know your dog wants to come back in? You find him waiting patiently at the door. This is your dog sending you that message. When you practice being in this quiet, peaceful place with an open mind, you can connect more and more with your dog on this mind level as they communicate with pictures. Once our minds are open, we can be aware of the pictures our animals are sending us. We can also send them pictures.

Step 2: Explore Your Pet's Past

Does your dog experience anxiety? Behavioral problems? Chronic bad habits? Health issues? Aggression? Depression?

Looking at your dog's past is very beneficial. It has been proven that our experiences can shape our behavior, beliefs, health, and decisions we make whether we are aware of it or not. Just like with people, when dogs have an experience, it makes an impression on them one way or another. When there are strong emotions involved, the imprint is that much more powerful.

My husband rescued a dog, and we named her Sera. Sera was extremely emaciated when she was found. She was very shy, afraid to be touched, and never barked. During the time with us, I did healing work on her and was able to tune in to her life of neglect and abuse before she came to our home. As she showed me her past experiences, I was able to do healing on those incidents so Sera was able to trust people again. Her behavior shifted and changed as she grew more confident and relaxed. Her physical health improved dramatically. Of course, she had quality food, a warm home, and lots of love besides the healing sessions. She started to enjoy being petted and she found her voice and was barking! It was wonderful to see her enjoy life and become healthier, happier, and stronger on all levels.

Over the years, I've done sessions on many different animals who've had a variety of experiences. When tuning in to the animal, they clearly show me and have me feel what has happened to them in the past. This can help their current owner understand the dog's behavior and how to treat him.

During the session, I also do healing work on the traumas or experiences of the past so they can resolve those old emotions and move forward in a different mindset. I help them update their mind and body to their current situation. This way they can fully enjoy their new home.

Certainly, there are particular behaviors or traits you will find in specific breeds, but each individual dog's experience is very important to examine. Often times, issues can be passed on from the mother or other relatives. This can be why a dog has problems even though they have a wonderful, loving home.

Experiencing healing/communication sessions help the owner of the dog to understand their dog better and can give them insight into what is most beneficial to their dog (i.e. what type of training etc.)

If the dog is carrying stress from his past, this can affect his immune system and eventually his health. Examining and healing the past can allow the dog to have the best quality of life possible.

Step 3: Look at Your Whole Dog

Often we hear the expression, 'it's just a dog'—meaning that they don't have thoughts, feelings, wants, or needs more than the physical.

Dogs are not only physical but also mental, emotional, and spiritual beings. As they become family members, it is good for everyone to look at them in this way. Even Pope John Paul II has declared that 'dogs have souls, too, just like men'.

When I tune in to a dog, I am connecting on a soul's level. As I feel what they feel and see what they see, I experience unconditional love but also jealousy, anger, sadness, and pure joy!

Bud was my first Chinese Shar Pei. We did everything together. We spent a lot of time training, entered dog shows, performed in festivals, exercised together, and had a lot of cuddles.

As I was going through a divorce, Bud was my protector and companion. He would know exactly when I needed some extra love and cuddles. He would let me know when I was under too much stress. He seemed to know me better than I knew myself during this difficult time. He kept me on track. I couldn't feel sorry for myself and slow my life down. Bud wouldn't let me. We were connected on that soul's level, and his unconditional love was very healing for me. It also helped that he was quite bossy so if Bud said something, I had to follow through!

When our dogs come into our lives, their purpose is to make us happy. Through sessions, I have seen dogs that go to the extent of taking on their owner's stresses, grief, etc., to help their owner feel better.

Our thoughts, feelings, and our bodies are energy. Our dogs are very aware of energy. This is how they can feel what we are feeling and take on some of this energy to relieve us and make us happier. Sometimes, the dog suffers if those feelings are too much for them. This can be expressed in behavioral, health problems, or other issues.

It is important for us to recognize our animals as these amazing, special, and complex beings when interacting with them. They are our best friends and are in tune with us on so many levels.

Step 4: Look at You

Our animals are watching us and very much aware of our thoughts and feelings. We have domesticated dogs and brought them into our hearts and our homes.

Often times, our dogs are more in tune with us than we are with ourselves. They take on our feelings or behaviors and act them out for us to see.

When I was going through a divorce, I was fighting with my ex-husband for what was due to me. At the same time, I was fighting for my rights at my place of employment. I lived with my family of four dogs and a cat. We were a very bonded and loving family, but my dogs started to get very cranky with each other. Eventually, they actually started to fight. I realized very quickly they were showing me what I was doing in my life.

Our dogs can be our teachers and show us what we don't want to look at in our lives. As soon as I made changes in my behavior, everything at home settled down and became peaceful once again.

So, when our dog's behavior changes dramatically, it's a good idea to look at ourselves and see how we are feeling. Ask yourself, "What is going on in my life right now?" Our dogs often mirror our behavior, feelings, and even our health.

It's important for us to look after ourselves—body, mind, and spirit—not only for ourselves but also for everyone around us.

Many times during healing/communication sessions, dogs will tell/show me issues that their owners haven't been able to look at or acknowledge. The dog knows that it needs to shift and change for the owner to be truly happy. I've had owners shocked and wondering how I know what I know about them. All the information comes from the dog.

This is why I refer to our dogs as 'angels on earth' because they help us learn and grow in so many ways.

Step 5: Look at the Environment

Dogs are aware and very sensitive to energies. This includes the energy of the environment around them. Their house (dwelling), land, neighbors, and, of course, the people and other animals in the house or on the property.

I was asked to come and do a session on a dog, Jack, whose behavior had changed dramatically. He used to be quite friendly but recently had been on edge and slightly aggressive, wouldn't sleep in the owner's room anymore, was pacing at night, and barking a lot more than usual.

When I connected to Jack, he kept showing me the roommate in the apartment. I started to smell smoke and feel quite depressed. He showed me how she was treating him badly when the owner was out at work. He was very concerned that she may hurt his owner, too. He felt sick from the smoke as well. He had me feel her energy and see how it was disrupting not only him but also his owner and the other animals in the house.

Jack's owner listened to him and had the roommate move out immediately. Jack's behavior changed overnight. He is now happier than ever! Having the session helped to get the roommate out of their space but also strengthened the bond and communication between Jack and his owner.

Belle, another dog I was hired to speak to had gotten very lethargic after her family moved into a new home. She wasn't eating well, didn't want to go for her daily walks, and wasn't acting like herself at all. Belle's vet ran many tests but nothing seemed to be physically wrong with her.

I asked to see Belle's picture and also a picture of their new house. When doing the session, I found out that Belle was tuning in to the energy of the house and it was making her very sad.

Through Belle and the energy in the house, I became aware of a traumatic event that had happened there in the past. I helped release all of the old negative energy associated with that event from the house and the land. I filled the house with bright, loving, light energy to cleanse and renew the property.

Belle and her family were all on holidays at the time of the clearing/healing session. When they stepped into the house, they knew something had changed dramatically. They realized that not only Belle had been affected by the energy of the house but the entire family. From that day on, Belle was back to her 'old self' and so was the rest of the family.

You now have steps of how to connect to your dog and look at them from a different perspective. Our animals have come here to be our companions but also so much more—our protectors, teachers, family, and angels on earth walking with us through this journey of life. When we connect on a deeper level with animals, their unconditional love is very healing for us. We learn to love ourselves unconditionally. As each one of us allows our hearts to grow bigger and gain more compassion for all the beings on this earth, we will shift and change the planet in a most wonderful way.

Mary's Special Offer

You now have five steps to look at your dog and what may be affecting his health or behaviour.

Start today to get your dog on track and living his life to the fullest!

Go to my page at www.DogHealings.com and sign up to receive helpful tips and call me for a free Discovery Session to see what is the best strategy for you and your dog!

Mary Stevenson 780-908-7685
info@maryestevenson.com

Mary E. Stevenson

Mary Stevenson is a Certified Clinical Hypnotherapist, Reiki Master/Teacher, Animal Communicator, speaker, and author.

A big animal lover, she has always been deeply in tune with people and nature. When she works on animals, whether it is in person or at a distance, they can feel the love and appreciation she has for them and freely communicate with her as she provides a clear channel to do so. There is a trust and an understanding at a deep level.

Through this connection using a variety of healing methods, she is able to help the animals change their behavior, improve their physical health, and enjoy their lives more fully. Harmony is created not only in the animals, but also in the home.

Her first book, bestseller *Ready to Love, Fact or Fiction?* (available on Amazon.com), is a guide to help people find the love of their lives. Based on her own love experiences and her training in counselling, she takes her readers through a journey of self-exploration which leads to a discovery of their authentic selves and creating the love life they have always wanted.

Mary was lead to holistic therapies during a physical illness. After going through a healing journey of her own, she knew she had to understand her own abilities and channel them into the professions where she could help others to heal as well. For the past nineteen years, she's been doing healing sessions, assisting people and animals to be healthy and happy and live life to the fullest.

A Final Note from Tracy Repchuk

Thank you for your investment in this book, and for the continuing relationship you will have with me and the co-authors.

We are dedicated to serving you and your needs and look forward to our journey together with you.

You can claim all of your free gifts from this book at www.MissionCriticalMessages.com. Simply enter your order # from Amazon and gain access to where all the author's gifts are located.

Enjoy the journey and stay in touch.

Connect with us on our Facebook page which has a link on your gift download page.

To Your Ongoing Success,
Tracy Repchuk
7-Time International Bestselling Author and Speaker

If you would like to become a published author and be in a book like this with me, go to

www.QuantumLeapAuthor.com

and take your next step.

Made in the USA
San Bernardino, CA
04 March 2016